MATERIALITIES IN ANTHRO

HOW WATER MAKES US HUMAN

MATERIALITIES IN ANTHROPOLOGY AND ARCHAEOLOGY

SERIES EDITORS

Luci Attala and Louise Steel
University of Wales Trinity Saint David

SERIES EDITORIAL BOARD

Dr Nicole Boivin
Director of the Max Planck Institute for the Science of Human History

Professor Samantha Hurn
University of Exeter

Dr Oliver Harris
University of Leicester

Professor David Howes
Concordia Centre for Interdisciplinary Studies in Society and Culture

Dr Elizabeth Rahman
University of Oxford

MATERIALITIES IN ANTHROPOLOGY AND ARCHAEOLOGY

HOW WATER MAKES US HUMAN

ENGAGEMENTS WITH THE MATERIALITY OF WATER

LUCI ATTALA

UNIVERSITY OF WALES PRESS
2019

© Luci Attala, 2019

All rights reserved. No part of this book may be reproduced in any material form (including photocopying or storing it in any medium by electronic means and whether or not transiently or incidentally to some other use of this publication) without the written permission of the copyright owner except in accordance with the provisions of the Copyright, Designs and Patents Act 1988. Applications for the copyright owner's written permission to reproduce any part of this publication should be addressed to the University of Wales Press, University Registry, King Edward VII Avenue, Cardiff CF10 3NS.

www.uwp.co.uk

British Library Cataloguing-in-Publication Data
A catalogue record for this book is available from the British Library.

ISBN   978-1-78683-411-9
eISBN   978-1-78683-412-6

The right of Luci Attala to be identified as author of this work has been asserted in accordance with sections 77 and 79 of the Copyright, Designs and Patents Act 1988.

MIX
Paper from responsible sources
FSC® C013604

Typeset by Marie Doherty
Printed by CPI Antony Rowe, Melksham

CONTENTS

Acknowledgements   vii
Preface   ix

PART ONE

1   Introduction   3
     The direction and purpose: New Materialities   3
     Materiality/Material culture/New Materialities   8
     Why water?   9
     People: bodies and water   10
     Agency   12

2   Water Behaviours: A Brief Ethnography of Water   18
     What is water?   18
     First light, then water   21
     Being liquid: physics, classifications, breaking the law and transformation   23
     How can one know water? Liquid behaviours   24
     The importance of movement: molecular sociology   25
     Solvents and solutions   29
     But *how* does water move? Circles, cycles and snakes   33
     The earth and the air   38
     Water: the shape of life, and when water is human   43

3   Resource or Source?: How to Approach Water in the Time of Climate Change   47

PART TWO

4   Introduction   65

5   The Giriama in Kenya: Living with Drought   68
     Water practices: rain, roofs, rivers and water basins   71
        Head carrying: water shaping gendered bodies   71

	Giriama conceptions of water	76
	Fu ha mwenga: fluidity and identity	76
	Watery identities	81
	Identity solutions: blending place, power and water	83
	MaKaya: home from home	86
	Giriama waters and authenticity: understanding the materiality of water	89
6	**Lanjaron, Spain**	93
	Slow water: glaciers, ice and snow	96
	The Moorish influence: hydrologers	99
	Invisible waters	101
	Not all waters are equal	104
	Mineral water: healing and destruction	106
	Change: festivities and water	109
	The ritual	109
7	**Welsh Water: The Resourcefulness of Water**	115
	Establishing Welsh water: then and now	117
	The language of water	119
	Discourses on deluge	123
	Water relationships, powers and control	127
	Memories of floods and flooding	129
	Water and memory: 'Remember Tryweryn'	134
	Reservoirs	141
	Yma o hyd (*Still here*)	142
8	**Concluding Remarks**	146
	References	149
	Index	169

ACKNOWLEDGEMENTS

The Wenner Gren Foundation has supported the fieldwork for some of the research for this book – under the title *The Role of 'New' Water in Shaping and Regulating Futures in Rural Kenya*.

I would like to thank: Sam Hurn, Louise Steel, Janet Burton and Ros Coard for listening to me bleat on about water for all these years; my students (particularly Kenny Lewis) for their bold and cheeky insights; Jane Cartwright, Steve Thomas and family, Rosemary Northover, Erin Kavanagh and Martin Bates for their help with the Welsh chapter; Tim Ihssen, who, after editing this, describes himself as 'an ugly bag of mostly water'; Sarah Lewis of University of Wales Press for this opportunity; my beautiful children, Kizzy, Minna, Llyr and Al, for being hilarious in so many ways, and for being the loves of my life and my absolute best friends; the ever-emerging grandchildren, who joyously demonstrate how materiality reshapes itself; Gary the cat, for waking me up before 6 a.m. because he was hungry and had to be fed *immediately*; the community in Kenya (particularly Alex and Loice Katana, and Musa Mare), who put up with my nonsense; and – last but not least – water, because, without you, we are dust.

PREFACE

This book is one of a series that contributes to what is broadly termed the 'new material' turn in the social sciences. The underpinning intention that coheres the numerous interdisciplinary moves that participate and feed into this flourishing body of literature is to challenge anthropocentricism. This series dethrones the human by drawing in materials. Positioned under the broad umbrella heading of the 'New Materialisms' or 'New Materialities', the series aims to draw in the non-human as agent, with a view to both recognizing and advocating for the other-than-human entities that prevail and engage in our lives.

In recognition that these terms are somewhat slippery to grasp, we have outlined the following distinctions so as to put clear water between the terms and to demonstrate how we are using them.

Distinctions between 'materiality' and 'matter'

The term 'materiality' describes the quality or character of the material of which a thing is made – what we might call its material-ness. On the other hand, the term 'matter' is used to describe physical items that occupy space (mass). Traditional theories of materiality explore how objects (made of matter (different materials)) shape the lives of people. New Materialities examines the materials (matter) of which objects are made and how those materials influence human behaviour.

Materiality and material culture studies have tended to focus their attention on *things* or *objects*, especially the things that people make. Scholarship has been less concerned with how materials behave, in favour of looking at how people use materials. Materiality studies, therefore, demonstrate a connection between humanity and the things that they make and use. In other words, it explores how items reflect their makers and owners, and therefore embody meanings.

The New Materialities turn moves away from objects and examines the materials from which objects are fashioned. Turning attention to the materials allows a new dimension to open up whereby the substance from which a thing is made becomes significant. Bringing materials to the foreground not only shows that materials are instrumental in providing the character and meaning of an item but also that the materials themselves determine – or are even actively responsible for – the final shape and manner by which the finished article can manifest. Thus, how a material behaves predicates how it can be used and, in turn, how we understand it. This perspective gives materials a type of agency both inherently and while in relationship with other materials. Indeed, using this perspective, it is how materials interact or engage that becomes the place of relationship, creativity and attention. Therefore, the NM draws into focus the materials of which things are made and, by focusing on the behaviours and characteristics of those substances, asks the question 'How do the materials (for which read "substances") from which we make things shape our lives?'

PART ONE

1 INTRODUCTION

The direction and purpose: New Materialities

This book is about how water becomes people – or, put another way, how people and water flow together and shape each other. While the focus of the book is on the relationships held between water and people, it also has a broader message about human relationships with the environment generally – one that illustrates not only that people are existentially entangled with the material world, but also that the materials of the world shape, determine and enable humans to be 'humans' in the ways that they are. Therefore, this book is first and foremost about relationships. It focuses specifically on water and, in doing so, draws attention to the liquid gossamer filaments that run through and physically join bodies and other matters, thereby foregrounding the part that water plays in shaping human lives. Through the adoption of what is broadly termed a New Materialities (hereafter 'NM') perspective (following: Bennett 2010; Coole and Frost 2010; Drazin and Küchler 2015) the inextricable links between the worlds of materials that people (as bodies) are part of are demonstrated.

An NM perspective is an inclusive approach to seeing the world (an ontology) that looks at how materials behave together so as to consider life from the perspective of material interactions. It intends to look past the boundaries that seemingly contain entities, to focus instead on how entities influence each other through their materiality. As with other approaches, an inclusive approach recognizes that all situations are complex, contingent, contextual and consist of multiple impacting influences (Urry 2005). However, by using an NM perspective, such complexities are seen to occur *within* the restrictions of being physical, rather than on other scales (for example, political or economic). It shies away from suggesting that just one aspect, method or manner has precedence over another, and in so doing it supports a move towards the appreciation of the co-generative aspects of relationships (or 'being together) to explore how relationships produce variable outcomes depending on the physics of all of the engaging materials. In short, inclusivity *includes* and, by including or relating to how more-than-the-human makes *the human what it is*, the NM approach avoids human exclusivity and discrimination against other aspects of the material world. In consequence, an NM perspective relates specifically to relationships (and almost their molecularity) rather than noting how singular items or individuals behave – that is: it explores (or brings to the light for inspection) the ways in which things relate to each other. Thus, it holds that it is the relationship (the manner by which things can relate) rather than the things *per se* (or exclusively) that is of interest.

The NM approach maintains that all behaviour and any possibility emerge from a material terrain, because there is no other 'place' where it can come from. Therefore to grasp the principles and influences that sustain and generate activities on any scale one must almost dissolve entities into their underpinning materiality to get to the core of how materials function, thereby realizing our fundamental dependency on the substances that form and constantly recycle themselves through us. By attending to the elemental bonds of existence, people blend into the world and any previously imagined separation is smoothed away. To grasp our unbreakable reliance and connectivity to everything else is the beginning of reshaping how we imagine ourselves, our actions and the vast material event of which we are part, symbiotically and with respect. Consequently, chiming with Ingold's notion of 'dwelling' (2000) that seeks to rematerialize people into the world, the NM perspective helps us to make sense of human life by directly challenging perspectives that rely on an ontological separation of people, things and stuff, which creates a perspective or way of thinking that disembodies people and presents them as though detached from the world through ideation. Where past methods have called for proximity and bindings to be realized, the NM perspective goes further, to strip away overlays of meanings that present humans as being anything but embedded in the material fabric in which all substances act as influencing co-shapers. In this almost 'jelly' of shifting materials there is no space or distance between things, because all substances are in touch with each other as a result of existing. Therefore, not only does the NM approach overcome the troubles of inaccuracies generated by the Enlightenment ideas that produced the categories, typologies and material difference that articulate current thought today (Attala 2017); it also relates to the Cartesian notion that exclusively attributes agency to people through the privilege of spirit and removes the tendency of modernist ontologies to favour the human above other sets of materials. Moreover, by logical extension, it forces the realization that we are all 'in this together' as a shifting set of materials without privilege over each other and that ecological justice relies on a future that recognizes our inherently shared materiality. How we design homes, use resources and produce goods, what we eat and how we engage with the materials that live with us need to be approached using this lens without which the calls for sustainable activities will be difficult to generate.

This approach draws the life of materials to our attention, so as to demonstrate that items (things or entities) do not exist in isolation or even separation but *are what they are because of the way they are able to relate* to other things (cf. Barad 2007). Therefore NM is a relational ontology that, by paying attention to the manner by which items relate and *can* relate to each other, illustrates that things can only be what they are because of the physics of any given situation. Wood, for example, cannot burn without oxygen to feed the flames, and people cannot live without water running through the cells of their flesh. How water becomes cells is determined by the behaviours of all the other materials or substances with which water must interact to get into and flow in the body. To use this approach, one must take an interdisciplinary leap so as to expose not only the physics of relationships but also the wider ecological network of existence (Ingold and Palsson 2013; Morton 2010). (The use of the term 'physics' here follows the definition of the word, and therefore concerns the *physical properties of matter*. It does not refer to the scientific discipline.) Once this leap has been taken, the shift in perspective allows the intrinsic material porosity of being alive to 'materialize', and it becomes possible to appreciate that items are not bounded or static but rather are fluid and in a constant state of flux, changing depending on what they are relating to (Capra 2002).

The overarching purpose of this approach is to encourage a fundamental reimagining of the world as one of materials in relationship with each other so that the illusion of people being separate from the material world is challenged. This intention is realized primarily through bringing materials clearly into focus as entities and not resources, but secondly by reminding the reader that people are utterly tangled with other materials because they are also simply an agglomeration of materials working together. This approach advocates the creation of novel interdisciplinary frameworks that promote a new analytic – one that encourages ethical, holistic and sustainable action (Bennett 2010; Coole and Frost 2010; Drazin and Küchler 2015; and Witmore 2014). This direction is therefore also designed to challenge representations that are blind to or repeatedly ignore (or sidestep) the fleshy materiality of being human in favour of remembering that humanity is distinctly *active with* and *part of* (rather than simply existing on) the fabric of the collection of materials we call planet Earth (Bennett 2010; Coole and Frost 2010; Ingold 2000; Iovino and Oppermann 2014). Moreover, without considerate treatment of the physics of processes, current dire forecasts of the unsustainability of human practices will be realized. Therefore, this highly political ontology advocates for a novel sensitivity to materiality that rejects the damaging illusion of separation that has paved the way for the recognition of differences and the discrimination that ideas of difference can promote and justify.

To see people as being disassociated from and simply users of planetary items relies on a mental or thought rift between the way in which people are seen and the way in which land, seas, skies, plants and so on are understood. Concerns associated with the perpetuation of this kind of intellectual schism between subjects arise with a sense of urgency in the Age of the Anthropocene – a time when recognizing the constant unfolding of materiality and our part in it assumes great importance because of the predicted risks associated with our actions. The mindset that assumes that people use the world fails to recognize that the world becomes people. Consequently, this book hopes to contribute to repairing any mental estrangement that permits people to continue to imagine that they are distinct from the world that *they live with and are part of*.

These days, it is increasingly common to hear how people are detrimentally disconnected from the natural world around them (Cohen and Duckert 2015; Keniger et al. 2013) and how this separation of people from the material world is the cause for our thoughtless, selfish and destructive actions in the Age of the Anthropocene (Cohen and

Duckert 2015; Iovino and Oppermann 2014; Morton 2010). While I have heartfelt sympathy for assertions of this kind, and on some level agree that many people live their lives *as though* disconnected from the material world around them, I am also aware, of course, that such assertions are nonsense. None of us can be (even just in terms of attitude) separate from the materials that we use because they are fundamentally a part of us – both physically and imaginatively. It does not take a large intellectual leap to realize that the flesh one articulates is simply composed of materials and that therefore it is utterly impossible to exist in any way other than 'materially'. However much we might feel or think that we are apart or distant from the world of materials, we are without question profoundly a part of it, and emerging constantly with it regardless of any technologies that manage to present an illusion of estrangement.

Some proclaim the importance of behaviour changes that reconnect people with the environment (Capra and Luisi 2014). Typically, these assertions state that humans must alter their activities so as to remodel their relationships with the natural world because current methods of engagement with the world are considered abusive, and that consequently a more sensitive and constructive attitude and model is called for. Again, I wholeheartedly agree, but that is not the primary focus of this book. Equally, it is not concerned with persuading readers to act differently. Indeed, in some ways, this book turns the typical broadcast environmental message on its head to show not how people should *use* water but how water is making them who they are. Consequently, by looking at what water does, I will demonstrate the part that the materials themselves have in shaping people physically, socially and culturally. Thus, the book adopts a perspective that foregrounds how water behaves to reveal just what water does, how it acts and how it is physically available, and therefore is dynamically responsible for the way that we can be human.

The purpose of this direction is twofold. First, I aim to repair the intellectual estrangement between people and the world of which they are part; and, secondly, by foregrounding water throughout the text I hope to illustrate how human lives do not simply need and use water, but are inextricably shaped by their relationship with it. I believe that this offers the chance for people to recognize just how dependent their lives are on other entities. Understanding that the different aspects of the planet are not here for our convenience and to (ab)use, we begin to see our relationship as parts of a bigger whole, and that the whole is using the parts (us) as much as the other way around.

Materiality/Material culture/New Materialities

The term 'materiality' should not be confused with a focus on objects or 'material culture' (cf. Miller 2005). Rather, the term 'materiality', in this case, is used to remind the reader of how objects/entities/bodies consist of a series of simultaneously interacting substances bound in relationship by physical laws (Barad 2003, 2007). The way in which the term 'materiality' is being used here chimes, to some extent, with Kohn's use of the term 'form' (2013, see chapter 5), which he uses as a baseline 'beyond the human' (2013: 159). He presents 'form' as 'a sort of general real . . . [in the] . . . self organizing emergent phenomena' (Kohn 2013: 159) of everything and despite any ambiguity considers it useful as a tool to conceptualize the material 'logics and properties' (Kohn 2013: 160) that shape us.

The foundation of the NM perspective uses a similar notion, but one that delves deeper into the very materiality of the shapes around us so as to elucidate how the substances that comprise and govern forms' patterns are tangled with humanity. Using this springboard, being human does not arise as a state divorced from material conditions (despite any depictions to the contrary), but rather emerges with and is informed by being integral to the behaviours of interacting ecologies (Capra 2002). Thus, as expressions of humanness are fundamentally predicated on the physicality of materiality, for accuracy, they should not be – and actually cannot successfully be – conceived of as separate or independent (Ingold 2000). Barad terms this error the 'Cartesian Cut' (2003: 815) in view of its perspectival, or intellectual origins in the work of Enlightenment philosopher René Descartes, whose machinist approach asserted there to be a distinction or a separation between materials and the thinker (mind/body dualism) (Descartes 1985). In calling for a reconsideration of the roles that materials play in making our shared worlds, it is necessary to illuminate the co-dependent relationships that construct and comprise the material world. This not only encourages a fresh, new outlook on what it means to be human (Bennett 2010; Coole and Frost 2010) but also forces one to realize that there is no separation between human actions, flesh, thought and the rest of the worldly substances that are in a constant state of flowing through us.

Why water?

As global agencies recognize the universal need to reconsider human–environmental engagement (Friends of the Earth International n.d.; Greenpeace International 2016; UNSDG n.d.), further information about water use and the meanings that it holds is considered to be of particular, contemporary significance (Fontein 2008). It is my belief that research concerning water that adopts an NM focus is better placed to contribute to current demands for the formulation of sustainable relationships with planetary resources than more traditional methods that depict water as a resource for human consumption without reference to the wider influence that it exerts. This is because depictions that explicitly realize the inextricably tangled chemistry of being human offer a clearer picture of the foundation of practices and thereby support alternative methods and solutions to be sought.

Currently, academic scholarship and global debates circling water typically focus attention on how humanity can most effectively use this common pool resource (Gleik 2014a and b). Thus, it is topics such as water usage, sanitation, hygiene, health and security rather than ecological and symbiotic relationships that characteristically frame discussions of water (Gleik 2014a and b). Viewed using an NM perspective, these traditional approaches to water can be accused of mandating (and perpetuating) a human exceptionalist outlook – a focus that NM challenges. Even studies that offer more nuanced understandings of water through documenting culturally contingent meanings of it, and give consideration to the socially generative potential of materials as they move into human lives (see Blatter and Ingram 2001; Wagner 2015), may not be enough. Simply to demonstrate that cultures have different beliefs and behaviours around water is undoubtedly helpful and interesting but, at this time in global history, I suggest that a more profound approach is what is required – one that moves away from seeking methods to improve human lives to one that seeks to improve the existence of all materials equally and together. At a time when information suggests that resources are stretched and physical forces are said to be dramatically transforming as a result of human activity, a fundamental shift in behaviours is cited as the only hope of maintaining the balance that supports life as it has come to be known (Morton 2010, 2013). As is probably clear now, this book aims to contribute in some small way to that shift. By using an alternative approach that explores and elucidates the relationships that people have with the materials that co-productively form them, I hope to draw out and highlight the material collisions and interdependencies that underpin sustainable existence. This book focuses on the activities of water and humans specifically and, with a pointed material focus, should also manage to move towards presenting the co-generative realities that human-materials have with *other* materials and beings. But this book could just as easily focus on people and other materials (cf. Attala and Steel 2019) as every material is in a profoundly physical relationship with us. In addition, because of our habit of reductionist thinking and the lexical support of that project, I am in some senses forced to present people and water as distinct before I can then successfully draw them together.

People: bodies and water

The theoretical perspective adopted here is grounded in a series of short ethnographic examples. This structure is designed to demonstrate how these ideas work and can be employed in different contexts. The methods help one reflect on how people are informed by (or materialized through) relationships with materials (in this case, water) and do not exist in isolation or without reference to a broader set of material influences. In just the same way as human behaviour influences water, this framework illustrates how water shapes humanity. The focus on water could be seen simply as a representational mechanism that blots and blurs the edges between human bodies and the material world in the text, but the intention concerns much more than simple representation. By highlighting existential corporealities with water specifically, it is possible to relate to the physical (or material) realities of human existence and thereby avoid the usual intellectual distance placed between bodies and the rest of the material world. Consequently, only through recognition of the very physicality of water and how it relates to people can the abilities of water to flow through and shape the contours of bodies, lives and cultures be explicitly and undeniably recognized and appreciated. Therefore, to avoid simply nodding towards water as an item necessary for existence, I hope to show not only that water is necessary, but also that we are the very water that we so regularly claim to 'need'. In addition, as the fundamental truth that our bodies are primarily watery moves away from being an abstract idea and towards being a material realization, there is value in asking where water stops being water and where it becomes a body or a person (Neimanis 2017). Consequently, if embodiment (that is, people being bodies) irrefutably relies on water being with us (or perhaps it might be helpful to state that we are water walking around as bodies), 'a radical question about what we mean when we call ourselves "bodies"' (Neimanis 2012: 83) emerges. Using an NM analytical framework that focuses directly on materials and their materiality allows one to approach this question head on. Thus, it is not just that water flows through us, or even that we need water to live, but that there is no clear distinction between when water is us or something else that needs to be attended to.

The ethnographic examples in this book are intended to support the aims above by encouraging the reader to reconsider their own relationships with water and, by extension, the wider environment and our collective places 'as' the material world. In addition, by looking at how piped and climatic water are variously understood, interacted with and used, this book offers an innovative perspective that recognizes a link, and levels the ground, between the shared human and non-human worlds – a position that is of critical importance at this point in global history (van Dooren 2016; Morton 2016; Tsing 2015; Witmore 2015). By centring on water in this way, this book will challenge the systematic division and ontological habit that situates water as separate from the (in this case, human) bodies that are primarily composed of it or that it becomes when in relationship with us. Moreover, it dissolves the notion that people use the materials of the world, in favour of seeing people *as* the materials that they relate to and have been presented as appearing to use. Theorizing water, as I intend to, elucidates its ubiquity and reveals that distinctions made between matters are unclear and inaccurate. In acknowledgement of this 'messiness', I intend to focus on fluidity of processes, avoid the 'cut and dried' and recognize the 'muddy' realities (cf. Appadurai and Breckenridge 2009; Lahiri-Dutt 2014 (Wet Theory); Mathur and Da Cunha 2014) that are implicit in relationships with water. In adopting this approach I look to move away from categorical and taxonomic models and oppositionals (such as wet/dry) to highlight how the performances of materials are relational processes of being.

There is an extensive body of literature that documents and recognizes both the significance of water as a 'conceptual lubricant' (Fontein 2008: 755) and the socio-political importance of water management and control (for recent examples, see: Chen et al. 2013; Fishman 2011; Gandy 2014; Gleik 2014a and b; Helmreich 2009; Palmer 2015; Strang 2004, 2009, 2015; Swyngedouw 2015; Wagner 2014). I intend to push past the work that demonstrates the role that water plays in human cultural lives so as to draw it in as a participant and generative agent. Much as non-human animals are considered to enable humans to grasp their humanity (Cassidy 2012; Haraway 2008; Hurn 2012), I maintain that so, too, should materials (like water) be recognized for the part they play in crafting what it means to be human. Furthermore, following the animal or multispecies turn that acknowledges that other living beings are significant social actors (and not just as objects) through which we can better understand ourselves, it is possible for water to be acknowledged as an active subject who becomes (with) us.

Agency

This perspective is one that advocates a wider definition of agency. New Materialists, using Latour's actors and actants in Actor Network Theory (1993a), recognize the inherent abilities of items to influence, provoke, incite, induce and determine behaviour as a result of what they are *made of* – not just as a result of their existence within a network (Bennett 2010; Coole and Frost 2010; Drazin and Küchler 2015; Witmore 2014). This definition of agency draws the material capabilities of substances to the foreground. Using this to explore water, its ability to flow, evaporate and stagnate etc., reveals how watery behavioural mechanisms predicate the way in which bodies and water can interact. While it might be helpful to assert that an item has agency simply because its capacities or affordances inspire or provoke one to act (following Gell 2013 and Gibson 1977), this definition tends to leave one playing 'agency table tennis', desperately attempting to locate agency within the human and then the object without success. Taking stimulus from the mechanics of theoretical quantum physics, agency is better understood as the intra-relational process whereby phenomena are produced from the field of possibilities that gel into matter when quantum forces engage (Barad 2003, 2007). Agency using this lens, therefore, is not a cognitive capability that is limited to certain species, but concerns the mechanisms of quantum processes that produce the materials of the world. From the perspective of quantum mechanics everything becomes as it does because of the mannerisms inherent in and prescribed by the methodologies enacted at the quantum level (Marletto and Vedral 2017). Quantum mechanics are not divorced from material realities. On the contrary, they form them (Marletto and Vedral 2017). Approached in this way, macro matters arise from the way in which micro particles can engage with each other, and the molecules formed from these relationships in turn produce objects and entities. Agency, therefore, cannot be embedded into only select items or conceived as a propelling thought process but rather may be more accurately conceptualized as a distributed mechanism that produces all things. Consequently, the methods of engagement that manifest at a quantum level are the shared agential forces that become material forms. Form therefore is representative of, and constitutes, the manner by which substances (or materials) are able to engage with each other (Barad 2007).

Thus, I adopt an eco-pluralist, hybrid theoretical framework that recognizes complexities (Urry 2005) and in some ways coheres the intentions of the animal or multispecies move (Kirksey and Helmreich 2010), the more-than-human turn (Bear 2011; Bear and Eden 2011; Kohn 2013, 2015; Whatmore 2002) and to some extent the ideas of posthumanism more generally, to highlight that existence and practice are fundamentally and materially relational and emerge because of the material capabilities and potentialities of relating agents (cf. Barad 2003; Bennett 2010; Latour 1993a). Hybridity rejects any focus on singularity in favour of the recognition of the complex 'messiness' of the relational multiplicity of engagements – in this case, the perspective is focused on the material agency of different types of water and the roles that they play in regulating cultural practices and the social relationships both between humans, and between humans and the rest of the material world. Consequently, the purpose of this cohered framework is to contribute to the levelling of the representational playing field following Latour (1993a) and Witmore (2014) so as to:

a) reject human exceptionalism as inaccurate and a problematic perspective that perpetuates an illusory separation between materials;

and thereby

b) re-present the importance of re-membering the existential entanglements and blurred boundaries between engaging material entities in the age of the Anthropocene.

As already noted, the theoretical purpose of this book hinges on the rejection of human exceptionalism in favour of a 'multi-material' plural perspective in which water and bodies are recognized as interacting materials shaping each other. Thus, through recognition of the co-productive relationship between water and people, I aim to demonstrate how water compellingly draws people to it and that, as a result of its vital material fundamentality and the concomitant biological insistence of regular engagement, water emerges as a formative, shaping component of cultural ideas and being human. Thus, using ethnographic examples, the multiple materio-cultural entanglements are explicitly and prominently – even blatantly – illustrated. Moreover, the examples clearly demonstrate not only the multiple existential dependencies with water that animate our lives, but also how materials engage to become what they are, and how those methods of engagement are predicated as much by how water behaves as by how bodies do.

Through the prioritizing of materiality we should be able to grasp a sense of our own physicality and the material influences that form what we are. In doing this the world is reimagined into a new shape, where what constitutes 'a person' is shown to be a shifting field of materials formed by the constant flows of the materials with which they engage. This perspective softens the rigid illusory barriers metaphorically encasing the human, which erroneously presents people as distinct and in need of protection from the rest of the material world (Douglas 1966), to reveal people emerging with the wider field of materials of which they are irrefutably and undeniably a part.

This book is structured in two parts. The first outlines the theoretical direction and purpose of the book, and offers the reader an ethnography of water: the second details water relationships in three different geographical locations. The structure of the book is designed to allow the reader to engage with the theory and then get to know 'who' water is, after which water relationships in different landscapes are used to illustrate how to use the NM perspective. Thus, because the way in which water behaves molecularly, its particularities and its predilections are briefly considered in the first part of the book, I have chosen to call this section an 'ethnography' of water, but I might also have called it a 'hydrography'. I chose not to, because the primary objective of the book is to demonstrate how water and people are inextricably interwoven and significantly co-generative; consequently, the title is designed to encourage the reader to see water and people as merged and to realize the right of water to environmental personhood.

The notion of environmental personhood is not one that transforms the environment into people or agents *per se*, but, rather, is one that recognizes the wider value of the planet. Used in this way, personhood is attributed to aspects of the landscape to which people feel an inalienable cultural connection. A recent example of this is the declaration in 2014 that the Whanganui River in New Zealand (*Te Awa Tupua*) has personhood. The attribution of personhood was established in association with the knowledge that local Maori ancestors exist as part of the river's water system. Consequently, the river now has rights, as do a number of other areas of cultural significance such as the River Ganges in India. In 2010, and in some ways acting as inspiration for the above attributions of personhood to rivers, the Morales administration in Bolivia passed a law that determines 'Mother Earth' in its entirety to be a person with rights (*Ley de Derechos de la Madre Tierra*; see Rightsofnature.org 2010), with varying degrees of success.

Using the basic tenets of applied anthropology, alongside notions of environmental personhood, this book could act as a document that, in part, could be seen to advocate for water. This is because the ethnography of water illustrates how it behaves and might be interpreted as something of a short introduction to the culture of water as a roving, transforming, shifting, mobile subject. I am not advocating for water. On the contrary, NM focuses on connectivity and relationships. Therefore I do this with a view to help the reader realize how our relationships with water are fundamentally important to being material and, therefore, to being human. To this end, the book reveals the diversity and complexities of (what might be called) the different cultures of water and therefore elucidates concerns of conceiving of water as singular (despite the term) – and suggests that water should be recognized perhaps as a collective noun, or an entity with multiple characters (just like people). Water's overarching aspiration to keep moving is a key recurring theme that is regularly revisited because it is a fundamental, physical fact that water urges to move on. In association, it is the different ways in which it ensures that it can mobilize in various contexts that force our hand and demand that we shape our lives around its activities. Furthermore, I show that it is because water must move that many of the biological processes of our bodies have been shaped. In other words, it is not inaccurate to state that people exist at the behest of water. But, of course, this is not simply a one-way street. Human bodies – as much as other materials such as the land, plants or air – are instrumental players or agents that impinge and impact on water's ambition to circulate. Bodies transport and relocate water in ways that other methods of passage cannot. Thus, bodies take water to places that it might not otherwise reach. Equally, the different ways that water manages to move are instrumental in the different ways that people have devised to be human. Looked at this way, it is possible to problematize the artificial lines drawn between the dichotomous oppositional notions of nature and culture, between what is deemed to be a body and what is a material, and between the idea of a subject and an object (Descola 2013).

The second part of the book illustrates the role that water plays in shaping various aspects of the landscape (including those individuals living within it) by exploring three different examples. These chapters explicitly illustrate how water's capacities, affordances and behaviours co-generatively shape human bodies and people's social lives.

The examples used here engage with water in contrasting environments and are designed to begin to illustrate the multiple manifestations of relationships that people have with water. Chapter 5 deals with drought conditions in rural Kenya and explores the social, physical and economic consequences of water insecurity in locations in which water supplies are irregular, inconsistent and sparse and where people are forced to perform regular, arduous daily activities in a bid to draw only very small amounts of water into their lives. Consequently, alongside its vitality, water can also be considered fickle as it constantly hides, which forces people to seek and find it.

Chapter 6 considers the role that snow melt plays in water systems in southern Spain. Through examination of another of water's capabilities, and specifically its ability to solidify in low temperatures, this section offers another example of the way in which water's materiality shapes lives. The ability to freeze is not exclusive to water, but its ability both to freeze and to avoid an increase in density while doing so is particularly significant. This section considers the role that 'slow' water plays in shaping people who live below the icy ridges of the Alpujarras in southern Spain.

Finally, our attentions turn towards a country renowned for its copious amounts of water: Wales. Chapter 7 explores water's ability to threaten, to deluge and to submerge, and considers the symbolic and political consequences of these abilities. It shows how the ability of water to flood geographies has been used as a political weapon, allowing those able to dam, hold and redirect it to retain power over those living on it. The chapter draws together water's materiality with national identities and demonstrates how the quiet drowning of a people's land transformed into a thunderous outraged roar that changed the course of history.

2 WATER BEHAVIOURS
A Brief Ethnography of Water

Water is a substance that people use every day, but most give little thought to it. We all drink it, cook with it, wash in it and use it to clean our homes without stopping to think about how it has got to us. Water appears to be 'just some liquid' that pours into lives when a tap is turned on, and, as a result of its customary familiarity, water is almost as invisible as it is seemingly colourless and transparent. Nevertheless, in recent years we have seen a surge of academic interest in water's recurring role in everyday life. This increased attention comes at a time of concern for the sustainability of worldly resources (Fishman 2011), and has promoted water away from a simple daily requirement or useful resource towards being a key player in discussions associated with health, hygiene and even modernity (Swyngedouw 2015). Moreover, with access to water now established as a human right (UN-water 2014), it also stands in the global public mind as a unifying principle for social justice.

What is water?

> How could [water] . . . be construed as life-less . . . and [be] defined as [an] inorganic substance?
>
> (Coats 2001: 113)

> The highest good is like water. Water gives life to the ten thousand things and does not strive. It flows in places people reject and so is like the Tao.
>
> (Lao Tsu 1989: 10)

In many languages, the word 'water' is an uncountable noun which describes a thing that cannot be divided or counted. Uncountable nouns are words that recognize multiples or collectives but also acknowledge difficulties in splitting the thing into parts. The use of the term 'water', therefore, presents it as a single substance, while the materiality of water offers a different picture altogether. As we will see in more detail later, water cannot successfully be thought of as one thing. Its composition changes constantly, as do its shape and density. Consequently, water would be more accurately represented as a transformational substance that shifts from one manner of being to the next – often rapidly and, certainly in terms of physical laws humanity has ascribed to the world, unexpectedly. Thus, to conceive of water as one entity is materially inaccurate and therefore problematic. Nevertheless, we use the word and, in doing so, make a distinction between what is water and what is not.

In addition, water is unhelpfully categorized as an inorganic compound in chemical or molecular terms. Despite a popularist view that such terms are useful descriptions that make clear and valuable distinctions between items, using the label 'inorganic' with regard to water is as problematic as assuming that water is one thing. This is because the definition of the term is troublingly ambiguous, as we shall see.

Living matter is based around what are called 'organic compounds', which are chemical partnerships that almost always contain carbon and are typically comprised of carbon and hydrogen bonds. Carbon-containing compounds form cells and consequently contribute importantly to biological or life processes being able to function as they do. As a result, all living organisms are defined as organic because their cells contain carbon. As we know, water does not contain carbon, as it consists of only hydrogen and oxygen atoms bonded together. Consequently, it is considered problematic to imagine that water is organic. According to orthodox definitions, then, it makes no difference whether water flows into and supports those biological processes to function, or transforms into an entity that is defined as organic: it remains inorganic. Using this method of categorization, a separation between what is organic and what is not has been produced, despite the confusing fact that organic compounds are composed of inorganic substances. Using these parameters with regard to water appears understandably problematic, not only from a New Materialities (NM) perspective but also from an orthodox scientific one, as the quote from Coats (2001) at the opening of this section illustrates. This is because water continuously flows through biologies, becoming flesh and phytomatter – among other things – and, therefore, it is quite patently present in living organisms. Consequently, when viewed relationally, defining water as organic or inorganic begins to be less helpful and may even lose meaning. Moreover, when using an orthodox, reductive and structural schema that categorizes the world as consisting of separate or distinct 'bits', the world begins to form into a certain shape – like a puzzle with pieces that need to slot together. Using a relational but also an NM approach means that portions do not need to 'fit' together, but rather slip and slide into each other with an amorphous fluidity – like paint mixing or the meal that emerges from the combination of cooking different ingredients together. Nevertheless, because, currently, water is viewed as an entity that is distinct from bodies – and because it is a molecule without a carbon atom – it can, rather misleadingly, be defined as inorganic.

Water's method of being is riddled with behaviours that can be considered to be ambiguities. It is as intellectually difficult to grasp hold of as it is empirically problematic to hold on to. In association, water is a vast, ungraspable complexity that exists in many places and in different ways simultaneously. For Morton, such entities are 'hyperobjects' (2010): things that are both singular and plural – objects and subjects, individuals and communities – concurrently and, consequently, are problematic, even baffling, to grasp fully when their enormity and irregularity are appreciated. For example, we do not talk of drops of water as independent water objects, or of a blob or drop of water as an object or a thing distinct from water itself. Like fire or air, bits of water are thought of as a part of a larger collective or community of water. This is what makes water so difficult to talk about, and it is why Morton has labelled it a 'hyperobject' (2010). Couple water's status as a hyperobject with its capacity to behave in ways that contravene our expectations, and then add its ability to generate life from the seemingly inert, and we have nothing less than an extraordinary substance.

Getting to know water (as if) ethnographically allows us to understand how it behaves, organizes itself and acts out its personality. Anthropology advocates deep immersion in a culture in order to get a grasp on how the system functions. For this reason, we are going to become deeply immersed in water so as to begin to perceive the enormous complexities, subtleties, struggles and requirements of being water. Once we have managed to see a broader picture of 'who' water is, we can go on to explore the relationships or cultures that water creates with people.

First light, then water

There was a time when there was no water – which means, despite any feeling that we might have that water has been a perpetual feature of existence, it has not always been around. The *possibility* of water appeared just a few seconds after the Big Bang occurred, approximately 14 billion years ago, with the explosive formation of hydrogen atoms. Indeed, the Big Bang produced vast, billowing clouds of hydrogen (a gas) – and, in consequence, even today, hydrogen remains the most abundant element in the universe. We need hydrogen to make stars. Therefore, we can hold hydrogen responsible for most of what followed. As readers will doubtless be aware, we need both hydrogen and oxygen to make water. Consequently, the initial clouds of hydrogen alone were not sufficient to produce water: oxygen was also needed. The production of hydrogen was simply the first step in what would prove to be a very long and complicated series of chemical and atomic dance moves between electrons and protons, cooling temperatures, and another 5 or 6 billion years would pass before oxygen eventually showed up.

In Classical thought, and in many other intellectual systems, water is presented as one of four or five elements, or foundations of life. For example, Ayurveda medicine places water alongside air, fire, earth and space as the foundations of the Earth, Astrology recognizes four elements (air, fire, earth and water), as do a number of alternative religions and shamanic schools of thinking. Equally, Cohen and Duckert's *Elemental Ecocriticism: Thinking with Earth, Air, Water and Fire* (2015) uses this conception of the elements as a springboard for discussing the potency of materiality, claiming that this method allows a move away from the 'mechanistic models that serve commodity capitalism well but licence environmental devastation' (2015: 5–6). However, despite the proclamation of the Greek pre-Socratic philosopher Empedocles (490–430 BCE in Leroi 2014), and others after him, when approaching water chemically it is incorrect to think of it as one of the elements. As Ball rightly reminds us, there is, in fact, no water atom (2002: 6). Water is, therefore, a compound molecule composed of two gases – hydrogen and oxygen – and it is often represented schematically as a shape that looks something like Mickey Mouse in silhouette, with the two hydrogen atoms as Mickey's ears. Hydrogen, the atom that, in the 1800s, chemists labelled the '"first matter" or *proto hyle* from which all matter is composed' (Ball 2002: 10), eventually managed to link with oxygen to form the molecular bond and pattern that we now call water. Rather than conceiving of it as something singular, we can now see that water is an amalgam or a compound of two atoms in relationship. At a very basic level, therefore, perhaps it is more accurate to visualize it as a manifestation of the relationship between those atoms – that is, an affiliation of atoms associating in such a manner that the material water comes into being. Looked at in this way, one can already get a sense of the potency of the NM approach – now that it is possible to appreciate that the very expression, and form, of planetary substances are predicated on a variety of relationships and how they can take shape (following Barad (2007) and Kohn (2013)). The format adopted by hydrogen and oxygen *is* the molecular relationship that forms or produces water. In Kohn's discussion on finding baseline generals by which to understand life, he asserts that it is form that generates 'constraints on possibility . . . [which, in turn] results in a certain pattern' (Kohn 2013: 158). Kohn is not referring specifically to molecular forms, but his point is still relevant as it makes one mindful of how the 'shapes' of being physical are determinants of what can follow. In terms of the NM perspective, Kohn's assertion on form is helpful as it allows one to get a hold (albeit a slippery one) on the brute reality of physicality and reminds us that materials adopt physical forms. In other words, even before an entity forms, materials must enact their relational processes and, in so doing (through coming together), prescribes and restricts the shape of future engagements and relationships *ad nauseam* in a kaleidoscope of burgeoning assemblages and reiterations of forms. In the case of water, the manner by which hydrogen and oxygen can bond, and the 'shape' that it then adopts, informs what water can be, and then sets its abilities to transform further. This is the case with all chemical events: water is no exception. However, water's capacity to transform and inveigle its way into alternative identities – from ocean to ice, from potato to bird, and from jelly to blood and back again – is remarkably flexible and productive.

It is this fundamental ability (even urge) to 'relate to' that is at the physical core of all materiality and life's myriad processes. By this, I mean, 'join with' rather than attempt to subsist or exist alone and as an individual. Without the partnership of the two atoms that produce water – and the material manner in which they can 'be' together – the extraordinary activity called 'life' would not have manifested as it has. Therefore it is not an exaggeration to state that the ability of hydrogen and oxygen to bond can be held directly responsible for life today, because it was their bonding that caused the condensation that was necessary to flood the Earth's still quite hot crusty surface with the first oceans. Rather poetically, just *how* water came to be on Earth is still uncertain. Under question is whether it formed in space (and was deposited on Earth via comets) or whether it formed in the rocks of the planet. Recent studies suggest that the water in comets is heavier than 'normal' water (and therefore is imaginatively called 'heavy water' (Hallis et al. 2015)) and uses a different isotope of hydrogen, called deuterium, to make itself, which means that, in all likelihood, the water on Earth was formed in the rocks deep below its mantle (Hallis et al. 2015).

As a result of the serendipitous relationship between the two elements, hydrogen and oxygen, grey clouds, rainstorms, mist, rainbows, rivers, tsunamis, sharp icicles, gentle snowflakes, enormous floating and land-gouging glaciers, steam and our cells – amongst numerous other things – developed. The power of water to shape the materials of the world, therefore, cannot (and should not) be underestimated or understated. Without water, life could not be sustained – but, equally, without water nothing would live. Furthermore, the physical manifestation or character of our planet would not be recognizable. It goes without saying, therefore, that there would be no oceans, rivers, streams or ice, but, equally, the shape or topography of the planet would be structured dramatically differently. Rocks would be jagged, no longer rounded by water's movement, and there would be no sand or mud – just rock and perhaps some dust.

Being liquid: physics, classifications, breaking the law and transformation

The scientific discipline of physics tells us that it is the properties of a substance that determine how it can behave. Here, the use of the word 'properties' describes the inherent attributes or qualities of the thing being described. Consequently, the properties of a substance not only distinguish and identify its feature characteristics but also give a glimpse into the behaviour or 'nature' of the material. Therefore, the somewhat mechanical mindset of physics as a discipline uses conclusions about the manner by which a substance behaves to establish the essential or intrinsic character of a material. By determining the character of a thing, one is able to understand something of it. Thus, using this method, physicists have been able to demonstrate that each type of molecule, atomic pattern, substance or material has something akin to a signature based on how it is able to behave within the rest of the fabric of the system in which it finds itself. This kind of information or knowledge has been considered useful across disciplines and industries – not so as to forge effective, equitable and sustainable relationships with worldly materials, but rather to know how things function or perform so that items can be used, altered or redirected into or out of human lives (Cohen and Duckert 2015). Thus, other than for the purpose of pure knowledge of the world, it seems that understandings of the physical workings of the universe are dominated by economics and the notion that knowledge must afford humanity an advantage of power to influence and thereby control materials for their own benefit. Using an NM perspective, the notion of one aspect obtaining an advantage over another is problematic, and indeed is simply intellectual and illusory, as the literature from the more-than-human movement aptly demonstrates (Whatmore 2002). In the short term, it may appear to be useful but, in the long term, such thinking unravels, because it is impossible for one feature genuinely to gain dominance within the wider whole of which it is part. Nevertheless, obviously, (like getting to know one's partner) knowledge of how materials behave is of value if we are all to live together well.

How can one know water? Liquid behaviours

> Water doesn't behave as it should. There are more than 30 physical constants of water that are 'wrong' . . . none of this can be understood by the common laws of physics . . . people will have to rethink their ideas about water.
>
> (Benveniste 2017)

As the opening quote to this section illustrates, water's properties are often presented as astounding by those who study and write about it.

What water does, and is capable of doing, is considered confounding to the physical laws that science has established, and that other substances prove to be restricted or held by (Ball 2002). Water can transform and renegotiate its methods of engagement in ways that mystify when compared with other worldly substances. Water, indeed, appears to be one of the most versatile and active materials (Chen et al. 2013). Put another way, it is a maverick material that is able to challenge many of the behavioural rules that people imagine they have discovered.

In a bid to classify and organize worldly entities, humanity has inscribed taxonomic categories on to the world. These categories vary from culture to culture but are always designed in such a way that they intellectually draw (what appear to be) similarities together by arranging the world into distinctly different or similar types of things (see Attala 2017). Most would agree that it is useful to be able to compare and contrast the properties of things to understand how they work. But, of course, the value of this way of organizing the world can also be challenged. As Kohn reminds us, 'difference is not the right starting point (2013: 158). In the case of water, this method of understanding proves to be particularly misleading and problematic. For example, water has been classified as a liquid because it behaves similarly to other substances that are defined as liquids. We may imagine that we understand what that label 'liquid' describes, but, on the other hand, it is possible that we are not fully acquainted with what the term means. Readers might assume that liquids are, well, *wet*. Unfortunately, they are not wet, and consequently, this means that water is not wet. Glass, for example, is a liquid, and it is not fluid in the way that water is. Water makes things wet – but being wet is not one of its capabilities, although it is part of the experience that one has when touching water. In other words, we get wet when we feel water, but being a liquid is not about being able to wet things. In the case of water, it just happens to do so. Being liquid is about movement.

The importance of movement: molecular sociology

> Matter is mobile, like a river; impalpable and elusive, like steam. It is . . . nomadic.
>
> (Consigli 2008: 101)

Being a liquid is about a particular type of movement. One could assert that material existence is more effectively characterized by attending to types of movement, because, despite appearances to the contrary, materials are never still: even rocks jiggle, at an atomic level. This means that every material item is in a constant state of flux and transformation and any sense of permanence, solidity or stability is a temporal illusion. Right from the wider movements of the universe and the planet spinning down to subatomic particles dancing together, materials are constantly shifting and rearranging, and, as particle physics clearly shows us, everything is vibrating and repositioning at different rates. Therefore, even items that are classified as solids are in fact molecularly mobile. Liquids – and their ability to move – lie on a spectrum between the two other methods of being (or movement): being solid or being gaseous. These different states of being are determined by the behaviour and arrangement of a substance's particles. To be liquid, the bonds between intermolecular particles must be loose and flexible, whereas, to be solid, particles must hold together more firmly. Loose intermolecular bonds create the characteristic fluidity that is expected of a substance that is defined as a liquid. More space and a lack of any particular arrangement create a gas, while a tight, rigid structure forms solids. With water, the arrangement of particles is fixed but loosely bound, thereby making it flow as it does, and allow it to be categorized as a fluid. Water's method of movement manages to retain the same density throughout the body of water – unlike a gas. Water's liquidity is not due simply to the hydrogen and oxygen particles forming adaptable or flexible bonds in a loose arrangement; the spatial properties, as well as the manner by which the particles relate to, or engage with, each other are of equal significance, as are the recent findings that 'water can exist as two different liquids' (Nilsson 2017). According to Pettersson, water is 'two simple liquids with a complicated relationship' (Stockholm University Press Office 2017) rather than one substance. This finding supports the notion that water fluctuates between different densities at room temperature. Consequently, 'water can exist in two different forms and ... the interplay between them could give rise to its strange properties' (Stockholm University Press Office 2017).

The spatial properties are also important, and so the manner by which the particles relate to, or engage with, each other is of significance. When hydrogen links with oxygen – when they both become water – they both bond faster than when in relationship with other molecules, and, perhaps more significantly, they are described as able to cooperate with each other when doing so (Finney 2004). Consequently, what Finney calls the 'molecular sociology of water' (2004: 1150) reveals that the atoms that assume the shape of the hydrogen dioxide molecules that are characteristic of water, have organized or arranged themselves using quite different methods from other substances. Therefore, when they are together, hydrogen and oxygen atoms construct relational bonds with each other in ways that other substances do not (Ball 2002; Finney 2004). Moreover, according to the laws established by the physical sciences, water behaves in unexpected ways and therefore should not perform in this way. Indeed, water really should not be a liquid at all. Strictly speaking, it should be a gas at ambient temperatures – but, obviously, and empirically, it is not. This physical rebelliousness prompts Finney to describe water's molecularity as 'inherently disordered' (2004: 1150) and, therefore, what one might think of as the key defining feature of water – that is, its liquidity – is described as being its 'anomalous liquid phase' (Finney 2004: 1150).

For a substance to be able to move as a liquid or as a gas does, the particles must be randomly spaced, and quivering or vibrating at high speeds. A loose internal arrangement, such as that just described, means that the particles – as it were 'within' the substance – are able to slide past each other easily. This is possible, in part, simply because they are not being held or confined in a rigid pattern by tight relational bonds. Therefore, if a substance can move, it is because the particles that comprise it are widely spaced and loosely bound while jiggling. Conversely, if a material freezes it is because low environmental temperatures affect the flexibility and arrangement of the particles by drawing them closer together, thereby making them even more tightly packed and rigid. In short, temperature affects the rate at which some molecules can move around. So, how does this affect water specifically?

It is common knowledge that water will solidify into ice when the temperature drops to 0°C or below. One could assume, therefore, that, when situated within such low temperatures, all water would first chill and then freeze. However, this is not the case. In keeping with its propensity for anomalous behaviour, water behaves differently. According to physicists Moore and Molinero (2011), water has been found unfrozen in clouds (that is, in liquid form) at temperatures below minus 50°F. This water, named 'supercooled water', refuses to freeze and remains a liquid, as though it has forgotten how to freeze. It is still unclear why this happens, but the fact that it does helps to account for why clouds do not freeze and fall out of the sky. Apparently, the introduction of ice crystals appears to *remind* supercooled water how to freeze, by setting off its freezing process on contact (ESRF.eu 2010). But that is not all: water continues to confound the laws of thermodynamics by freezing more quickly if hot than if cold. This is called the Mpemba effect, after the student who discovered it in 1963 (Jeng 2005). If that were not enough, water also behaves differently from other solids when it is frozen.

Materials that are considered to be solids are expected to have a higher overall density than liquids or gases, because of their tightly packed particles. When liquid substances freeze they are said to solidify and are expected to increase in density and effectively shrink in mass, through drawing the particles together. Thus, we know that most substances shrink with cold and expand with heat as each atom takes up more space as temperatures rise – but this is not the case for water. When water transforms into ice, it expands until it freezes. Indeed, with regard to solids and solidifying generally, water's behaviour stands in opposition to expectations or physical laws again: it first expands and then lightens in density rather than constricting and becoming denser. Thus, as temperatures drop, where other substances force their particles to become more tightly arranged together, the hydrogen bonds in water act so as to push its particles further apart, thereby creating more 'space' between them, and seemingly enlarging as it freezes. That is why glass bottles filled with water shatter if left in the freezer for too long. But extra space between atoms has consequences other than spatial. It also functions to lessen the density of the ice being formed, in comparison to any water around it. It is this perverse behaviour of water that allows us to have ice floating in our drinks on hot days. And while transforming into a solid that is lighter than the liquid version of itself is another startling achievement, water's abilities do not stop there. Compared with other materials, water is remarkably difficult to heat up. Readers may have already noticed that it takes a lot of energy to boil a kettle to make a hot drink. This is because of the rate at which water absorbs heat (Coats 2001: 112). If water had a lower specific heat point, our (and other plant and animal) bodies would be dangerously affected. This is because rapid increase and decrease in body temperatures would encourage our flesh to decompose or, conversely, freeze up, in accordance with the temperature of the water in it. Just to add more confusion to this – equally bizarrely, drops of water are able to last longer on a metal plate at a temperature above 100°C than on one that is cooler.

The above section briefly outlines some of water's abilities that fail to fit into the categories that we have created to understand the materials of the world. First, we have noted that the bonds constructed between hydrogen and oxygen are inherently disordered and behave differently from other molecules. Secondly, how water behaves when it freezes contradicts the patterns of behaviour that are displayed by other freezing substances. Water expands rather than contracts when frozen, thereby allowing it to float and preserve life in lakes under it. Conversely, there are some circumstances – for example, at high altitude – where it simply will not freeze. In addition, the enormous amount of energy that it takes to heat water is partly responsible for the existence of biological life. As such, water presents as an extraordinary maverick material with remarkable capabilities.

Solvents and solutions

> Water's appearance does more than just trick us into believing it to be material purity. Still water reflects and excited water splashes and waves.
> (Wilkens et al. 2005: 14)

As we have seen, it is water's atomic relationships that enable it to move as a liquid, a gas and, when hardened into a solid as ice, to float in a liquid form of itself. Labelled the 'hydrological cycle', these transformational abilities allow water to circulate the planet, transmogrifying and inveigling itself within diverse bodies to ensure its own perpetual rotation. It can move upwards through evaporation or as steam (gas); downwards, as condensation in the form of drops (of rain); it seeps into things; it moves through bodies osmotically; it bides its time as ice; it cracks open rocks in which it freezes and it allows other entities to take shape by plumping up the cells of plants and animals, before cleaning out both collecting and depositing materials as it goes.

Most liquids can dissolve substances in them, but water is claimed to have the greatest dissolving powers of all of them (Ball 2002). Indeed, water is hailed as the universal solvent, as most (but not all – see, famously, oil) substances dissolve in it. Thus, water is the ideal material mechanism for reorganizing substances and earthly matters at both micro and macro levels. Indeed, in its relationship with the topography of the planet, its capacity to hold dissolved items means that water is persistently transporting multiple materials, and in so doing it recycles and redistributes materials from one location to another without prejudice. It is as though water is 'blind': it sees nothing and so judges or rejects nothing.

Furthermore, despite the appearances of adverts designed to sell bottled water, it is quite wrong to imagine that water is ever pure, and it certainly is not empty. Water is full – teeming with microscopic particles and living beings (Helmreich 2009), unless it has been treated. Water's fundamental lack of material purity has not restricted its identity as the archetypal cleanser and as a generic cleaning substance. Indeed, Parkin cites water as a cross-culturally recurring idiom for cleansing both spiritual and mundane realms (1991). Water washes things away and, in so doing, removes – that is, through its capabilities it makes other items move on again. As has been covered previously, where water is left to its own devices, not only does it fill itself but it also moves into and fills spaces whenever it can. Wherever it flows, water dynamically interacts with whatever it meets, and, using its ability to carry things in solution, it remodels whatever it is liaising with. That water is so ready to pick up and embrace what it comes in contact with means that it cannot be pure water without interference. However, with interference, it can be deemed 'ultra-pure' if it goes through multiple filtration stages to draw out anything that is not either a hydrogen or an oxygen molecule. Ultra-pure water is a ferociously effective cleanser because it is empty. Its being void of the 'stuff' that it usually plays with means that it rapidly scours what it comes in contact with, hungrily drawing any particles into it and away from the item being cleansed. Drinking 'empty' water is terribly dangerous and would not be recommended, as it would eventually kill us, because its consumption strips us of nutrients as the water attempts to fill itself up with the nutrients inside us. Ultra-pure water is used in the construction of microchips for phones and computers, as it can thoroughly clean up these tiny areas without doing damage or harm to them (Fishman 2011).

The human preference for living on dry ground may have encouraged the portrayal of oceans as spaces of separation that cause problematic distance between land masses. If we shift the perspective to one that recognizes water's materiality, it is possible to view water as the material that joins land masses rather than separates them (Rainbird 2007). The ability of water to merge is evident at multiple scales, and, as Wilkens et al. (2005) remind us with regard to clay, 'Water holds particles together making them soft and pliable' (2005: 21). The ability of water to move and dissolve planetary matter in solution is the mechanism that not only forms connections but also, through linking vastly different land masses, enables items (microscopic and much larger – think of boats) from one location to be transported to another. In connection with the ability to blend itself with other entities, water problematizes the distinctions made between empty and full, complete and incomplete, and space and place – and, in so doing, reminds us of the problems of the language borders that sit as though between ideas separating them. As was seen above, water is still water despite being full or empty of other things. It remains water despite these changes to its composition and therefore when an area is labelled muddy it is difficult to determine whether it is saturated soil or water full of earth. Furthermore, just as air invisibly occupies space, and it is simultaneously conceived as not there or a space (or the gap) between things, water is both the space (distance between) and place between land masses. Air is not thought of as a thing in a place (Edgeworth 2011). Moreover, it is held to be nothing everywhere. Rather like the amusing and popular black and white drawings that play with perception to demonstrate that, in the same picture, people will be able to see different items – for example, either a young or an old lady – water can be determined as occupying space but also as being the space, as being simultaneously present but also one of the hybrid ingredients of an item.

In addition to its abilities simultaneously to transport, transform and ambulate in the many ways mentioned above, water also soaks into other materials, filling them up. By flowing into other materials, water's transportation mechanisms are also utilized to bring items not just across distances but also *into* bodies. Therefore, its exceptional ability to incorporate dissolved substances makes it inordinately suited as a medium of communication and of connectivity between what appear to be disparate items. Water embodies a continuous process of 'give and take' that exemplifies relationality in action on a grand and global scale. Water is literally materially ungraspable, but equally water itself clutches at nothing – instead, through eddies and swirls, it takes, circulates, communes and distributes what it can.

As we have already noted, water's liquidity is typically held to be its primary fundamental form. Thus, ice, steam, snow, sweat, blood and so on lie in a somewhat liminal space, being both water and not-water simultaneously. Seen in this way, water can be depicted both as a series of different materials altogether and also as being able to transform itself, depending on conditions. It seems that we are not quite sure how to understand water, and this highlights one of the key points of the NM approach: that when we refocus our attention away from singular entities we see the world as consisting of constantly shifting materials in a wider network or blending field, and not as separate 'things'. To hold on to this thought means that it becomes difficult to ignore what Morton (2010) and Ingold (2011) call the 'meshwork' of which all materials are part. In any event, it transpires that, when someone uses the word 'water', predictably, we think of a liquid, and, in part, forget that it can shift into other forms. In recognizing that I am slightly sidestepping the issue at hand – that is, water becomes virtually everything – I want to turn attention to its identities as gaseous and solid characters, because both are noteworthy and thus should not be overlooked. We touched briefly on frozen water earlier, but let us take a closer look at ice and steam, and understand the significance of being able to shift into these forms. Without the ability to rise both through the air and through bodies, using the processes of transpiration, respiration and osmosis, water would be stuck, inhabiting the lower grounds. (The term 'bodies' describes forms including all cellular life (human animal, non-human animal, plants and so on), but equally the bodies of materials such as wood, paint, shells, horn, plastic, etc.) Without its ability to freeze, the planet would be too warm and liquid water would evaporate, causing the atmosphere to become more dense and the world to become hotter. Water's ability to move up enables it to use gravity to flow down again, which means that the planet is coated with, soaked by and run through with circulating water.

Therefore, it is not just the fact that water can move that demonstrates its contrary nature, but *how and when it can move* that makes it exceptional and signatory. Of significance to us here is that all these rule-breaking behaviours are what make water vital and central to life as it currently manifests itself. In other words, these are not inconsequential behaviours but the key characteristics that produce life as it is here on Earth. Indeed, if hydrogen did not bond with oxygen in the way that it does, life (as we know it) would not exist today. The fact that ice floats, and the fact that water freezes from the top down, are both key to enabling aquatic life to survive in low temperatures. This, coupled with the warmer water at the depths of the oceans, has allowed underwater life to thrive and be transported around the planet regardless of external temperatures (Helmreich 2009). Furthermore, water vapour in the air is considered to be the principal greenhouse gas on our planet, and any reduction in evapo-transpiration rates, through, for example, deforestation, can shift and alter weather patterns dramatically (Bartholomew 2012: 119). More than that, the hydrological cycle functions by using water in all its three forms (gas, liquid and solid) simultaneously – a cycle that nicely illustrates how water rejects constriction or containment, and is permanently on the move – despite any appearances to the contrary.

But *how* does water move? Circles, cycles and snakes

> Wherever water occurs it tends to take on a spherical form. It envelops the whole sphere of the earth, enclosing every object in a thin film. Falling as a drop, water oscillates about the form of a sphere; or as dew fallen on a clear and starry night it transforms an inconspicuous field into a starry heaven of sparkling drops.
> (Schwenk 2014: 13)

As we have seen, water insists on moving not just at a molecular level, but as a substance – flowing and pouring through bodies and across geographies. As we also now know, its molecular structure is what enables it to do so, first because of its inherent fluidity and secondly because of its capacity to transform into other things. As a liquid, it is a combination of the collective weight of water in association with gravity and the movement of the planet that are the key driving forces that propel water to move. However, water's flexible molecularity also has another profound property: interestingly, water molecules have the urge to be spherical, and it is their urge to be spherical with the pull of gravity that determines *how* they can move.

Watching water in space (where gravity has no influence) shows how water forms into amorphous blobs, glooping around in the air rather than flowing vertically as we are used to, as when it emerges from a tap, falls as rain or flows in a river. This arises as a result of the relationship between surface tension and how the water molecules have the urge to bond when there is no gravity. When water molecules bond it is as though the body of water produces something of a boundary to it – what we might call a skin or edge. This 'skin' is created by the molecules' intention to form the smallest possible area when joined, thereby creating a 'bit' or blob of water. This is what makes drops of water form, and it is these characteristics – not in isolation, but in relationship – that account for the different ways in which water is able to move.

That water moves is evident. It is palpably evident with regard to many of the manners in which we engage with water: tap, river, stream, ocean waves, even steam and drops of sweat reveals water's drive to travel on. Furthermore, across the land, and even on what seem to be flat planes, water appears to have an uncomplicated, unidirectional flow. Readers might have noticed that rivers do not flow in straight lines. The reason for this concerns its internal spiralling movements. The water looks as though it is simply flowing but in fact its manner is not fully uncomplicated or unidirectional. Water not only moves as a body within the river channel through which it is flowing; it also spirals within itself as it does so.

> Rivers do not run straight for more than ten times their own width, which means that if you find one that does you are looking at evidence of human tinkering.
> (Gooley 2016: 80)

The internal 'spinning' of the water describes the motion that it adopts as it moves through a water channel. It is this method (of being) that produces the characteristic serpentine shape that rivers gouge out of the landscape. The technique results from the internal revolving core of the water, which is produced by water's incessant urge towards being spherical in relationship with the other physical forces already mentioned. Thus, rivers are able to snake through and dig down into the landscape – not simply because of erosion and deposition, as we are taught in school – but because the water within the river banks is constantly attempting to form a sphere that is being stretched out by gravity and its own weight. It is these relationships that create the 'sinuous, convoluting' (Bartholomew 2012: 142) circuitous configurations of rivers.

The inner working of the flow motion of water is mostly invisible, but it can be seen at the edges of streams. If one gives attention to the water alongside objects such as rocks or the bank, one can see the spiralling pattern that water adopts as it navigates around them. Any movement or turbulence in water causes the totality of the body of water to respond and flow in accordance. Thus, water moves as an interconnected unity and, because of its constant internal spiralling, it reacts to even 'linear stimuli with rhythmic ... eddying motions' (Wilkens et al. 2005: 28). Looking at how water moves in planes, we can see that it not only flows down the river, and simultaneously eddies around objects in the water, but also generates longitudinal vortices within the body of the water around which currents of water revolve around each other (Schwenk 2014). These vortices, like liquid drills, are responsible for the deposition and erosion of a river, and are the process by which the path that it forms bends, which, in turn, is responsible for the direction the water takes as it drills its path into the landscape. Thus, meanders are 'the expression of the rhythmic flow of water' (Bartholomew 2012: 22) and enable us to visualize how water moves when it is a river. These intertwining, inner spiral patterns of water can easily be seen in the steam rising up over our coffee cup or in the water going down the bath's plug hole. These spirals are stretched out or elongated examples of water's urge to be spherical.

The processes of deposition and erosion are significant not just for the direction of the river flow, or for the shape of the river channel and landscape, but also for the continuously reorganizing shape of the internally coiling body of water moving within the channel. Temperature also plays a part in organizing the shape of the water, because warmer water tends to deposit its cargo more readily than colder water does. This means that streams with warmer water are less able to carry what is held in solution and, consequently, accumulate sediment and silt up more readily, thereby causing the contours of the river to change rapidly. As tree roots act like refrigeration, keeping the banks cooler (Bartholomew 2012), rivers lined with trees are effectively cooler than those that are not. Rivers lined with trees are therefore less likely to silt up and cause flooding by bursting their banks. Consequently, rivers that run through open fields or towns without being tree-lined could be more prone to flooding because of the small amount of extra heat held by the water (Bartholomew 2012: 159), and no amount of barricading will suffice to inhibit this process because the flooding is not the result of extra water exclusively, but is the consequence of the combination of water temperatures and its method of movement in a given setting. Furthermore, meandering – as a river does – is a method of 'putting on the brakes' (Bartholomew 2012: 166). Without this behavioural pattern, 'heavy masses of water would over-accelerate, rupture the river banks and cause immense havoc' (Bartholomew 2012: 166) – a pattern of behaviour that is increasingly seen in urban locations across the world today, where water courses are dammed or reshaped into systems designed to serve human conurbations. Adjustment to river ways, particularly those adjustments that attempt to straighten the course, and that fail to account for the essential vitality of the water, will be unable to 'hold out indefinitely against the "will" of the water' (Schwenk 2014: 18). Indeed, according to Schwenk (2014), the health of water is determined by its ability to move, and any process that fails to recognize its urge to be spherical and its resulting spiral behaviours (such as a typical urban water system) within the wider physical system of relationships is likely to cause unintended adverse consequences.

This type of mechanism is, of course, evident in all waters, including the oceans. The oceanic gyres, whose method of circulating results from what is known as the Coriolis effect (the pattern of movement created by the drag associated with the westerly spin of the planet), produces obvious and visible evidence of this spiral motion from the currents but also from the accumulating plastic waste that is circulating in huge, watery spirals in the five major ocean gyres. In similar ways to the water in rivers, the ocean currents massage the underwater topography, coastal edges and beaches, albeit on a different scale. The character of ocean waves is also illustrative of water's urge to be spherical, as each crash on to the beach or sea wall and each curl of the waves demonstrates. These actions produce multiple circular movements that intersect and penetrate each other, which create a series of watery vortexes or 'moving part[s] within a moving whole' (Schwenk 2014: 46) that have been compared to an 'organ' (Schwenk 2014: 48) constantly churning within the body of the ocean so as to distribute its cargo and reshape its passage. Therefore the movement of the water in the oceans is vital for circulating material substances and items in solution, but this is not its only function; it is also vital for regulating planetary temperatures.

Ocean waters play a vital role in regulating the climate and the weather. This is not simply about sun-warmed water moving around the planet but is because of water's ability to absorb gases – carbon dioxide, in particular. When ocean water meets the air it forces any carbon dioxide into solution, along with the other solids it is carrying around. Rather than simply carry the carbon dioxide across locations, the water's circulating motion sends it down to the deeper layers at the bottom of the sea, where it sinks and can be stored and remain in stasis for many years. The ability to absorb carbon dioxide is an important behaviour that not only supports its ability to dissolve other solids for circulation but also facilitates the reduction of atmospheric carbon. Absorbing carbon infinitesimally heats the water. Therefore, large amounts of carbon dioxide in the water raise the oceans' temperatures. However, as the temperature of the water rises, its ability to absorb carbon reduces, which in turn diminishes water's mobility and its capacity to absorb any more carbon (Riebeek 2008). The further consequences of this, I am sure, need not be laboured. It suffices to say that the anthropogenic carbon emissions that are currently peaking at a record high are thought to be threatening the oceans' ability to move and to cycle carbon as they once did (Riebeek 2008). Moreover, hot seas – that is, sea surface temperatures over 82°F – coupled with cooler winds, have the propensity to escalate into serious and destructive meteorological disturbances such as hurricanes, as recent events in South America and the United States have demonstrated.

The above illustrates the inherent relational intimacies between water's behaviour and the other aspects of the landscape and the atmosphere that it moves with and through. The focus on movement is key to understanding what water is, what it does and that it must do what it can. We have seen that, when moving as a river, water simultaneously produces a horizontal current of water (as it engages with gravity) and contains an inner spiral of water within it while it flows. This means that, within the body of water, multiple concurrent activities are taking place that shape the material – first, the water moves downstream, secondly, it flows in waves that eddy up against obstacles in its path, and, thirdly, it produces a spiralling vortex that drills into and deepens the path along the river bed. These simultaneously functioning mechanics of water are part of the set of processes that contour the earth with which bodies of water engage. Each body of water uses the same mechanisms to move but presents with its own morphological character on account of the different environmental factors with which it is in relationship. Water, therefore, presents as an immensely complicated but tremendously flexible – even adaptable – material presence.

The earth and the air

Throughout the text so far, I have laboured to remind readers to think in terms of relationships and connections rather than isolated, singular items that are split or detached from each other. This is in conjunction with the NM approach and the attention that it gives to how materials interact or relate to each other. As has been outlined, this focus has been inspired by Barad's (2003) assertion that it is as though between what *seem* to be discrete things that activity – even agency – is taking place. In keeping with this, let us turn our attention to the place where water and land very obviously interact, and in so doing illustrate the problems of considering materials as separate or distinct from each other.

The term used to label the interface between the land and water in rivers is the 'riparian zone'. The term typically focuses on the land that meets the water (and not the other way around) and it is presented as a buffer between the two different types of materiality. The plants that grow in this wetter area are described as 'hydrophilic' (water-loving) and are thought to stabilize the bank, stopping the water from disintegrating and collapsing the edges. The riparian zone can be extensive and, increasingly, such areas are being protected to support conservation and biodiversity. The edges of the riparian zone form a muddy or blurry region in which a relationship between water and earth occurs. This is where the material intra-activity between both entities arises. 'Intra-action' is a neologism coined by Barad (2003). Her term is useful to us because it recognizes how relationships produce the elements that are relating and also because it supports recognition of how relationships produce them. In this case, not only are the boundaries between substances blurred; how each material contributes to the making of the other through mutual engagement is also 'visible'. Continuing with the example of water flowing as a river should help us to visualize this. Let us imagine the water that is in contact with the earthy banks actively picking up and depositing 'bits' of the coarse surfaces that it is streaming past. In doing this, river water becomes full of river bank or 'earth' (for lack of a better term). Similarly, the earth running along the river soaks the water into it, making the earth that constitutes the boundary of the river or the land's edge saturated. As a consequence, the water or land's edges are both full of water and earth, making it difficult to say accurately which is which at this point. Moreover, when this is recognized, the boundaries that we intellectually construct around objects or materials (in this case, around what is water and what is land) become significantly choppy, physically muddy and troubled. Indeed, these physical places of contact problematize, and should make one question the mental depiction of each aspect as distinct from the other – because, quite simply, it is just too difficult to delineate successfully where one starts and the other stops. Furthermore, this demonstrates that using a relational ontology to approach material relationships is a helpful method to draw out and understand the subtleties and characteristic porosity of materiality articulating the formation of the world and reveals the 'reality' (following Kohn's notion of form (2013)) and purpose of attending to intra-actions rather than to *inter*actions.

Following the same logic, we should also consider water's relationship with the air as another illustration of how its transformative qualities manage to enable it to both lie between and simultaneously blend with what is around it. Not only is water positioned physically (in broad terms) between the seemingly solid land and the gaseous air; it also penetrates and is present in both concurrently. Water therefore manages to blend with items considered either solid or gaseous, which results in its managing to blend all three categories, as the following demonstrates:

> Every waterfall dissolves at its edges into an infinite number of the tiniest droplets, forming an inconceivable extent of surface at which the two elements meet and there water surrenders itself to the air. The opposite process may be observed where water cascades and pours over stones into a pool. Air is then swept into the water, sparkling bubbles and creating great surfaces of contact at with the water can 'breathe'.
> (Schwenk 2014: 102)

From the above, we can see that water is never *just* water and that, from the many 'waters' available, all water(s) are different. Consequently, while water is water it is also air and the earth. Moreover, as Bartholomew (2012) reminds us, the world of water is one of motion. We can see that water does not remain still if left to its own devices. Without respite or enervation, water continually has the urge to spread, shift and relocate. Consequently, it forms the bodies that root into and mobilize through the soil, air and liquid versions of itself. Other than running through everywhere and getting its liquescent fingers into each and every nook and cranny of the planet, it also joins everything by producing a running, flowing network between lives. Liquid water bashes, drags at, shakes up and absorbs the materials around it, so as to pick them up, transport them and later deposit them in other areas. Equally, frozen water cracks open and grinds off sharp edges, and atmospheric water accumulates and redistributes materials across landscapes. These materials can be either microscopic or of tremendous size, and as a result have the ability to alter lives utterly – as both disease transmission and tsunamis effortlessly illustrate. It is this multiplicity of methods and manners that makes water the mistress of multitasking – and what makes water so difficult to grasp in totality (cf. Morton's hyperobjects (2010)).

As the above illustrates, it is difficult to find the physical boundaries of the substance that we label 'water' successfully – or, in other words, to know where water stops or starts. Boundaries can be erected intellectually, and language manages to contain water conceptually, but, when approached chemically or materially, finding the beginning or end of water becomes much more problematic. Nevertheless, the substance that we call water is also utterly apparent and available to us, and is evident phenomenologically in the different ways in which we experience it. Consequently, the ideation of 'water' as a distinct entity subsumes its physicality to emerge useful, persuasive and utterly internalized, and, because of this, has rarely been up for question. However, simply on the basis of brute chemistry, the description or classifications of water as a singular substance need to be challenged. As seen through this lens, then, water is not *a thing, or even just a material*.

By way of a reminder, from a material perspective, water is a process or a method of becoming and dissolution: it is simultaneously human and other lives, animate and inanimate, subject and object. In addition to these complications, just as with all other materials, water cannot and does not develop in isolation, but rather forms because of, and through, its intersecting relationships with surrounding influences and other substances, which means that one can say that we are as much human as we are water.

This method of representation is not designed to present water as mysterious or exotic, although when one looks at the fluid in this way it is hard not to be enchanted by its transformational abilities, its influence and the diversity of its expression. Rather, following Latour (2014), this method remind us of what is irrefutably there: a field of materials without 'edges' that, through relationships, become the 'things' that we perceive and name. There is nothing more or less than this field of engaging materials shifting together in relationship.

> Earth is neither nature, nor a machine. It is not that we should try to puff some spiritual dimension into its stern and solid stuff – as so many romantic thinkers and Nature-philosophers had tried to do – but rather that we should abstain from de-animating the agencies that we encounter at each step.
> (Latour 2014: 15)

Consequently, the examination of water's chemical behaviours and the subsequent problems of classification (Attala 2017) outlined above are drawn into discussion to demonstrate one of the core articulating themes of NM: things are never entities in their own right because they are always composite beings formed because of multiple on-going coinciding, co-productive, dependencies in elemental association at *a material level*, and because items can only come into being themselves as a result of their material relationships. Therefore, by scrutinizing the abilities of materials, as the NM approach advocates (in this case, the material is water), it is possible to illuminate and problematize the way in which water is understood as an entity in its own right, and therefore to demonstrate the indestructible connectivity between materials and what we call people.

Remember: the NM perspective is just one approach among many that can be held under the umbrella term 'relational ontology'. As the name implies, theories that class themselves as 'relational' are concerned with how relationships produce the existential terrain that articulates everything. Rather than looking at items of the world in isolation in order to understand them fully, relational ontologies focus on engagements and connections and maintain that relationships are the mechanism by which everything is generated. Advocates of relational ontologies are also critics of Enlightenment-inspired reductionist methods. Relationalists maintain that to envisage the world as consisting of separate entities is a destructive, inaccurate fallacy that needs to be challenged.

Therefore, the NM perspective should not be seen as one that reduces the world to one of materials but rather as one that looks to relationships through a material (almost molecular) lens so as to extend the reach of examining how relationships can manifest and are enacted, and to demonstrate the internal mechanisms essential to materiality that produce influence and agency. Moreover, current ecocritical rumblings also attribute the establishment, perpetuation and feeding of an illusion of material disconnection (Cohen and Duckert 2015; Iovino and Oppermann 2014) to reductionist methods, and are concerned that this illusion emerges from the schools of thought that classify and present materials, things, people and other beings as being both taxonomically and physically distinct from each other, when *in fact* they are existentially tangled, co-generative and mutually dependent (Cohen and Duckert 2015; Coole and Frost 2010). Remember, as Kohn told us earlier: 'difference is not the right starting point' (2013: 158). Using an NM focus, the fundamental 'general real' (Kohn 2013: 159) that Kohn is seeking tangibly emerges out of the substances as they cohere into forms. Using this perspective, the illusion of lives being lived in division as separate things blurs away, allowing only a field of potential and possibility to be evident (Barad 2007).

Once the internalized cognitive scaffolding that encourages us to think of ourselves as separate from the materials that become our flesh breaks down, and the reality of being in a material field is brought to the foreground, one should become unable to perpetuate imaginings that place people at a distance from their actions and their effects, and any myopia that blinds us to the damage that we do to *ourselves* (as material(s)) should also dissolve. Once this realization fully takes hold, we will be enchanted by how we and water exist together and by what water does both to (in)form us and shape our experiences. By drawing us closer to the materials from which we are fashioned, the intellectual distance diminishes, and thoughts of items or objects can be replaced by those of processes, relationships, blendings, becomings and porosity – not as abstract, theoretical ideas about practice, but as ones that are actively and physically grounded in 'the general real' (Kohn 2015: 159).

Water: the shape of life, and when water is human

> Existing things have no nature – only a mixing and separating of what has been mixed. Nature is a name given by human beings.
> (Empedocles cited in Leroi 2014: 80)

Water's ubiquity allows it to feel familiar to us but, as has been illustrated, so far, most of us are unfamiliar with some of its abilities. Moreover, if we are to think in terms of relationships, defining water as a material that acts on, and as a substance that is distinct from, other materials, rather than one that *acts with* them, becomes problematic and difficult to continue. As we have already noted, when conceived of in these terms, water is not *a* thing but is simultaneously multiple utterly different things acting in concert: as blood and intercellular fluid, it is bodies; as clouds and fog, it is air; as juice, it is fruit or vegetables; and as mud, it is the earth. Water is flexibility personified; it is the epitome of versatility and transformation, existing as one and many because it is 'in a constant state of motion' (Coats 2001: 113). However, despite being the key component to life's forms and to life forming, water is not characterized as being alive. Water lies somewhere between inanimate and animated.

> Water does not have the characteristics of the living, but without water there is no life . . . water does not have the expressions of life, but these all only become possible through water . . . What is it that enables water to accomplish this? By renouncing every self-quality it becomes the creative substance for the generation of all forms. By renouncing every life of its own it becomes the primal substance for all life. By renouncing every fixed substance it becomes the carrier of all substance transformation. By renouncing every rhythm of its own it becomes the carrier of each and every rhythm.
> (Schwenk in Wilkens et al. 2005: 26)

For Schwenk (in Wilkens et al. 2005), it is not water's adaptability or transformational capacities that make it extraordinary and powerful but its refusal to be entrenched or to retain a position. Water renounces a form, manner and method in favour of slipping into many forms, manners and methods. Other than as a molecule, water manifests with no essential shape prerequisite. Therefore, collectives of water molecules adopt the shape of the things with which the fluid finds itself in association or relationship. Consequently, the items that make up the river banks (rocks, stones, roots, and so on) define the shape of the body of water coiling or drilling through the space as a river; similarly, the shape of water in a cup mirrors the shape of the receptacle it is in, and the shape of a cell or the circulatory system confines the shape of the fluid in it. Thus, water adopts the shape of the thing into which it pours itself, and, in so doing, can be understood of as filling the space. The example of water in a cup is one in which the cup's edges force the water to describe the shape of the cup by filling it. However, this is not the case with all other items. Water moving into items can also shape them. Fascinatingly, as every emerging life form passes through a liquid phase, many solidified biological forms reflect the swirling movement of water's spirals. For example, the architecture of bony objects, such as shells and horns, assume a spiral in design, as do microscopic entities such as DNA, chromosomes and spermatozoa (Consigli 2008: 93) – just like the shape of moving water hardened into form. Equally, the fleshy materials that make up our corporeality follow similar patterns. For example, the human heart is essentially formed of an elongated tubular spiral that is twisted around itself, which not only mirrors water's method of movement but also supports the blood in moving effectively (Schwenk 2014). Brains are similarly constructed. In addition, 'the spiralling form of muscles . . . bear witness to the living world of water' (Schwenk 2014: 24) and 'bone has raised a monument in "stone" to the flowing movement from which it originates' (Schwenk 2014: 25). Indeed, for Schwenk, it appears as though 'the liquid has "expressed itself" in the bone' (2014: 25). Thus, the movement described by water flows are evident in the very fabric of matter (Schwenk 2014). Therefore, not only does water take shape; it also shapes or acts on other materials. Thus, bodies and their vessels reveal an echo of watery patterns in their composition.

> and we soon recognize ourselves as watery bodies among water bodies, all sloshing around in a watery world.
> (Neimanis 2012: 86)

As the above hydrographic information illustrates, water, just like humanity, is complex, perverse, surprising, law-breaking, magnificent and, most significantly, unrelenting in its intent to make its way around the world. Water's cycle is well established in our minds. We know that it moves from the oceans up into the clouds, which then allows it to rain down on to mountains, flow into rivers and back to the sea, only to start the process again. We are taught in school that this is what water does, and this cycle is offered as an explanation for how water gets around the planet. However, the way in which the cycle is represented typically places its movement at a distance from our flesh. Left out of the picture is the fact that it runs into and through our bodies as well as the landscape and air. Finding variously sized exit holes across the surface of our skin, water uses our perambulating flesh to redeploy itself from one location to another. Indeed, if we were to push this perspective to its limit, we could assert that, through the use of pipelines, channels, aqueducts, reservoirs and such (constructed by people to bring water to their lives), water has managed to spread itself into areas that it otherwise would not have been able to influence. Therefore, when it is in the form of a human body, water has not only constantly re-engaged with water sources, but has actively constructed mechanisms that continually enable it to replenish its supply of itself. Water flows with and as people as much as it does as clouds, oceans and glaciers.

Consequently, depictions that intractably continue to present water as distinct in its existence from human lives perpetuate the intellectual distance between the physical materiality of being alive and the ontological method of thinking about being alive. Representations that illustrate how bodies are inextricably watery encourage an alternative perspective on what life is and support a reduction of the gap placed between what we think we are and what we are materially. Reducing the 'space' between what it means to be human and being material forces the realization that what is done to materials is simultaneously done to our bodies.

3 RESOURCE OR SOURCE?
How to Approach Water in the Time of Climate Change

> Water gets into our perception by bloating, flooding, and colouring the world.
> (Wilkens et al. 2005: 14)

> To Influence:
> 'A flow of water, a flowing in,' from Medieval Latin *influential* . . . The range of senses in Middle English were non-personal, in reference to any outflowing of energy that produces effect, of fluid or vaporous substance as well as immaterial or unobservable forces. Meaning 'exertion of unseen influence by persons' meaning 'capacity for producing effects by insensible or invisible means.'
> (Online Etymology Dictionary 2018)

This section moves away from a hydrographic exploration of water to think harder about how water and its behaviours have been conceived of, studied, depicted and presented. In doing so, this section will draw the relationships between water and people ever more explicitly together. This section also allows us to become familiar with current interdisciplinary methods of representing water – as resource, as material, as symbol, as agent – ethnographically and cross-culturally, and will act as a review of some of the different perspectives or approaches to water that are used across academic disciplines.

As we have noted previously, scholars have had a tendency to study objects or items in isolation – in a bid, they claim, to understand them fully. This section will build on the tone of the previous ones to demonstrate the value of rejecting a separatist approach in favour of knowledge that emerges through the relational lens advocated here. The framework for this perspective weaves together a number of theoretical threads – namely, the multispecies ethnographic approach, more-than-humanism and posthumanism (see Barad 2003; Bennett 2010; Chen et al. 2013; Kohn 2015; Latour 1993a and b; Whatmore 2002 as examples of these directions) so as to contribute to the repositioning of foci that current interdisciplinary scholarship calls for. In privileging materiality (in this case, specifically the materiality of water), it is possible to begin to tease out not only the value of conceiving life as comprising blurred, wet, spongy or porous relationships but also the important consequences of doing so. Furthermore, drawing the world as one interactive entity into view, instead of isolated bits working to survive over others, highlights the ethical and political significance of this approach, and illustrates how the New Materialities (NM) approach does more than expound, explore or elucidate relationships.

Extensive attention has been given to water in diverse disciplines, which has established it as a vital substance, an inspiration, a tool and as a resource (Shaw and Francis 2014; Strang 2004, 2013a). As a resource, discussions around water security, supply, storage and ownership abound. Thus, numerous texts explore the politics of water from the perspectives of control (Coopey and Tvedt 2006; Strang 2013b; Swyngedouw 2015; Thomas 2013), while others relate to seeking the technological and scientific solutions necessary to ensure an enduring and secure supply (Gleik et al 2014b). As readers will have probably realized by now, that is not the focus of this book.

> We are really facing a global crisis . . . demand [for water] is predicted to outstrip supply by 40 percent by 2030.
> (Boltz, science and environment lead at The Rockefeller Foundation, talking about water – cited by Rowling 2017)

Presenting water as a resource seems sensible enough. After all, all of life (including, of course, human lives) relies on regular access to a supply of water for its survival. And, during a time when 'water is proclaimed to be the next global crisis' (Blatter and Ingram 2001: 3; and see Rowling (2017) and WWAP (2018)) discussions that relate to ensuring the sustainability and security of supplies are apposite and crucial. However, primarily associating water with the notion of a resource is also intellectually limiting, and potentially destructive, for numerous reasons. The first is that it places a substance that relies on a movement principle of cycles and circulation into an industrial system that is designed upon reductive notions of cause and effect rather than the (currently advocated for) methods that incorporate ecological complexity into their structures (AGWA 2018; Capra 2002), and the second is because it foregrounds and perpetuates the notion that people are separate from the rest of the worldly materials. If we can get away from the fantasy that imagines that the world can be used for human purposes solely, and move towards representations and designs that embrace and advocate for shared materialities, not only will sustainability be achievable, but it will also be woven into practice as the norm (Capra and Luisi 2014).

Capra (2002) reminds us that the Latin root of the word 'resource' is *resurgere*, which, originally meant 'to rise again' or 'to spring forth' rather than 'a stock of items stored and available for use', as it does today. Thus, its previous meaning might have been a useful label for water, as it poetically chimed with what water does or how it behaves. However, today, describing water as a resource means that, instead of identifying watery behaviours (i.e. springing forth), water is now established as a human requirement – as an item that people need rather than a being in itself – and, furthermore, is associated with the countless other stockpiled or hoarded materials that are bottled or packed and held in readiness for human consumption. It was only relatively recently (in the 1700s) that the term changed meaning and became aligned with economics and wealth. This form of categorization, however, produces more than a simple economic position; it is also a strong ideological position in which trade and the control of resources are 'equated with the lofty idea of human freedom' (Capra 2002: 230). Framed in this way, water easily emerges as a commodity in a system in which its value is conflated with cost:price ratios, rather than other measurements of worth. Needless to say, a perspective that calculates water's value predominantly through its connection to human lives necessitates the development of management policies and technologies to ensure water's effective containment and distribution for human use, and pays cursory attention to what water needs or its intrinsic value.

The obvious, but also important, question to ask here is: 'Who is water being managed for?'. Perhaps you have answered that easily. I expect that you might have said: 'For humanity . . . of course.' And, this would be a reasonable answer because societies need to ensure that the land is watered for agriculture, that water flows into homes for domestic purposes, that excess water can drain away and that property is able to deflect and guard against any watery advances. However, having noted that the relational ontology and framework for this book emphasize that people are positioned within a boarder ranger of ecological relationships and do not exist in isolation from the material world (Ingold 2000), favouring humanity begins to look problematic and troubling.

Moreover, as water cannot be claimed to be one thing any more, we find ourselves presented with a linguistic, representational and ontological conundrum. If we maintain that water management and security involve a discussion about humanity's survival, rather than about how to relate to water to ensure a more-than-human biophysical, broader understanding of survival, then the systems we create will fail to take into consideration the character and needs of water. Furthermore, if we are to take Schwenk's ideas (2014) concerning water's character and behaviours into consideration to continue to prescribe and interfere with the principles of movement water uses will detrimentally affect the health of water and, consequently, will detrimentally affect our materiality and the rest of the world around us. Humans are just one of the many geological agents that are actively engaged in producing and maintaining life, and as such the geomorphology of being human indisputably and emphatically emerges through its relationships with water (and other materials). Thus, in light of the water crisis that is purportedly looming (Rowling 2017; WWAP 2018), any discussion on security, management and distribution must also relate to the inherent connections inextricably entangling between interacting parties for it to be sustainable (AGWA 2018).

Similarly, from a cultural perspective, Blatter and Ingram (2001) are most emphatic that new methods of approaching water are necessary and overdue:

> We insist that the researcher must first understand the meaning of water as it exists in a particular local place or social context.

Only then can the scholar apply specific explanatory approaches. This priority given to understanding leads us to propose specific methods that concentrate on the social construction of meanings of water as well as that of identities and preference of actors and communities.
(Blatter and Ingram, 2001: 4)

Their statement affirms the need to acknowledge and include different meanings explicitly and specifically, and is illustrative of the ongoing interdisciplinary scholarly discontent with regard to how to approach water and other materials (cf. Coole and Frost 2010; Drazin and Küchler 2015; Ingold 2000; Kohn 2015). Their perspective acknowledges that there are a variety of ways in which to understand water; while this is undoubtedly of great value, it does not push the boundaries far enough, because it still relies on a human exceptionalist framework, in which human needs transcend other requirements and balanced relationships are rarely under consideration. Simple recognition of a variety of meanings, while useful, therefore still lies shy of the focus that I propose here.

On the other hand, in acknowledgement of the timely importance of a holistic comprehension of water's role in the landscape and the intersections between diverse species within geographical settings, global agencies now recommend that future designs of water governance should draw inspiration from natural processes and should not focus on human demand and hygiene needs exclusively (AGWA 2018). In contrast to past methods, current directives now suggest that designs of water systems should be structured with the ecological needs of the biophysical totality of the locale in mind. In short, solutions to water problems should now be 'nature-based', designed collectively and for each context individually if they are to ensure ecological and geographical balance.

> Nature-based solutions (NBS) are inspired and supported by nature and use, or mimic, natural processes to contribute to the improved management of water. The defining feature of NBS is, therefore, not whether an ecosystem used is 'natural' but whether natural processes are being pro-actively managed to achieve a water-related objective.
> (WWAP 2018: 25; see also European Commission (n.d.))

Thus, in the last few years, there has been a bold paradigm shift from representations of water as an economic resource for human use exclusively to one that realizes the broader set of material relationships in which water takes part, which has provided new thinking about water that chimes with the overarching intentions of the NM. Furthermore, this shift asks for discussions to reject the notions of water scarcity and productivity as its articulating themes, in favour of sharing, commonality and wellbeing as project goals. In a time when methods have been judged as lacking and when innovation is hailed as vital, novel methods of engagement with water are refreshing.

One reason for the failure of past methods is that the designs of water systems are shaped around the idea that water must be controlled if they are to deliver a regular supply of water to people effectively. In contrast, NBS advocate an ecological design that stresses that water systems must be developed locally, use indigenous knowledge and be decentralized and managed at the lowest level (Mitsi and Nicol 2013). Further, such designs should incentivize conservation, improve soils and encourage biodiversity if the water is to be fairly shared with all entities living in the environment (Mitsi and Nicol 2013).

NBS, therefore, are, by definition, hybrid solutions, emerging as a result of collaboration at all stages from all agencies involved. They use diverse ideas and mix methods from other locations to form the process that works most successfully for an area's ecological requirements. As a result of this 'no-size-fits-all' situation, each region will be expected to design a system to fit with the environmental needs contingent to the area. NBS are flagged as being able to contribute significantly 'to solving or overcoming the major contemporary water management problems and challenges' (WWDR 2018: 22), but are also recognized as being useful in improving water and encouraging biodiversity in areas without considerable problems, including urban locations (see Horizon 2020 report on 'renaturing cities' (Directorate-General for Research and Innovation 2015)).

How water is managed shapes people as much as it impacts on water's behaviours and abilities. Thus, current thinking is making moves away from presenting water as a resource and moving towards making representations that place water into a wider set of ecological relationships. Moreover, to present water as a resource that humanity must use without consideration of what water needs is to ignore the materiality of relationships and erroneously interpret water as an inert necessity and an incidental rather than co-productive agent and partner in the generation of humanness. When approached using a framework of relationality that recognizes the multiple influences and distributed agency of existence, we need to ask what water systems could look like if they are to be symbiotic, as NBS expect. If we noticed how water wanted to move, would we construct straight watercourses or pipes for it to flow along? If it were recognized that rivers lined by trees were less likely to flood, would care be taken for trees to be planted along them? If we were to approach water as being materially embedded within ecologies, would we drain it from one area to provide another, dam it and restrict its passage, and would its role in the lives of non-human animals be on the table in discussions of global water security?

Using an NM approach offers a fresh method to engage with the brute physicality of ecological relationships. Such an approach draws people into the world of materials and uses that as the baseline for understanding change and development. By relating to materiality, this method avoids placing people at a distance from the substances with which they engage, by holding people (or bodies) as one of the sets of engaging materials circulating, coalescing and influencing the wider ecology of relationships that collectively form the landscape.

Anthropological and philosophical approaches to water liberate it from the narrower confines of economics, technology and resource use, to produce a diverse body of work that demonstrates a wider variety of ways in which to engage with and understand the cultural consequences of this vital fluid. Strang and others (cf. Strang 2013a, in Chen et al. 2013) – following Levi Strauss's notion that humanity intellectually uses aspects of the world to produce meaning to live by (1964) – have shown how good water is to think with. By explicitly recognizing and paying attention to how water's materiality or behaviours are enacted, they show how water has inspired people to think about it. That is: people use its wateriness symbolically and metaphorically to explain and account for their own behaviours. Indeed, the plethora of literature that explores how water is good to think with has itself been illustrative of how easy it is to soak the text with puns, as one babbles on about water. As a result, there are extensive accounts that comprehensively illustrate the many ways in which people draw inspiration from water's physical presence and its behaviours (Strang 2004; Wagner 2015).

In conjunction, there is also a wealth of literature that shows the significance, and cultural shaping powers, of water (e.g. Ball 2002; Carse 2010; Carey 2010; Fishman 2011; Gleick 2014a and b; Lansing 1987; Strang 2004, 2009, 2010, 2013a and b, 2014, 2015; Wagner 2015), and all of which contribute to a tremendous body of information and demonstrates the variety of meanings associated with water. However, discussions that establish water as a culturally and symbolically significant material, without considering the many ways in which the material properties of water physically shape human actions and choices ignore the 'humans-are-materials' component of material relationships and perpetuate the perspective that water is a material that people use and think about rather than think-with (cf. Levi-Strauss 1964).

By explicitly acknowledging the material connection between physical bodies and water, discussions are able to move away from the depiction of water as a contested, controlled resource and towards debates that relate to the part that water plays in ordering human–hydrological relationships. As a result, the separation between 'things' on which traditional representations rely is problematized and the inherent 'muddiness' and messiness of being human in a world of materials are allowed to rise to the surface. Taking inspiration from Lahiri-Dutt (2014) and Appadurai and Breckenridge's (2009: ix) call for a new wet(ter) theory that softens the hard edges that dominate our thinking, this perspective recognizes flux, flows, contingency and insecurities rather than seeking out firm boundaries, straight lines or dry land to stand on. Furthermore, just as wet theory is spongy and soaks up ideas from context, using this perspective foregrounds that people do not use water, as is commonly misrepresented, but, rather, live in relationship with water as it runs through their bodies. As a result of this relational, co-productive and interactive flow, the false dichotomy that is commonly established between what is natural and what is cultural can also be challenged.

Debates concerning how to use the terms 'nature' and 'culture' successfully are too numerous to discuss here in any detail. (For a comprehensive overview of how, when and why a binary relationship between nature and culture was established, see Descola 2013.)

However, water's part in problematizing distinctions between what is nature and what is cultural does need to be attended to, briefly. Discussion of the fallacy of the nature/culture divide has been extended to include the part that water plays in the rhetoric and infrastructure of (post)modernity (Appadurai and Breckenridge 2009; Fontein 2008; Gandy 2014; Hughes 2006; Lahiri-Dutt 2014; Strang 2004, 2009, 2015; Swyngedouw 2015). For example, Strang uses water to illustrate how any division between nature and culture is simply conceptual (2015, 2016). Stating that humanity's relationship with water altered dramatically with the movement away from foraging to farming, she maintains that it was agriculture that motivated the development of 'intricate methods of managing hydrological flows' (Strang 2015: 74). Not only did this produce different ways of relating to the environment; it also encouraged new ways of thinking about materials and other species. Indeed, for Strang, early irrigation methods of relating to water therefore represent

> a quantum leap in human societies capacities to control their material environments . . . Indeed, it could reasonably be said that the control of water, more than anything else changed humankind's relationship with the other species on the Earth and asserted the primacy of human agency.
>
> (Strang 2015: 86)

It is difficult to know exactly which point or place in history Strang is describing, but nevertheless the activity of damming and holding water in position has regularly been interpreted as one of humanity actively demonstrating its control over the environment (a point that will be returned to again in detail in Chapter 8). For Strang (2015), damming water is an obvious indicator of culture in action, because it is assumed to be a human activity that overtly shapes the 'natural' or 'wild' water and harnesses it for human use. However, she also notes that water systems simultaneously problematize the arbitrarily placed divide between nature and culture, because water physically flows in and out of cultural spaces. From an NM point of view, however, it is the facts that water can be dammed, how it behaves when it is dammed, and how damming shapes both people's lives and water itself that are of interest. Rather than imagining that people use water, the NM perspective explores how water and people blend and shape each other through the ways in which they can be together. By adopting a relational approach, the processes of damming water can be repositioned as products and effects of the inherent possibilities of an eco-material relationship (which cannot be attributed to either cultural or natural behaviours effectively) between water and people, and is evidence that any intellectual division between where nature stops and culture starts is not only artificial but also limited in meaning (Descola 2013).

The materiality of water, therefore, further troubles the social constructs and the ontological boundaries that have been erected by language. The fact that water can be and is dammed is instrumentally influential and has shaped people's ability to engage with it in multiple ways. This in turn has directly altered not only landscapes, but also thinking and people's bodies.

So, how should one think about water?

> Into the same river you could not step twice, for other . . . waters are flowing.
> (Heraclitus (*Fragments* V 13, 10) 2013: 10)

The quote from Heraclitus is more commonly translated as 'one cannot stand in the same river twice' – a statement that, in referencing the behaviour of water, manages simultaneously and aptly to evoke the material character of the substance. In essence, this quote reminds one that change and movement are paradoxically constant with water, despite any appearances of consistency and stillness. As we have seen, the physical characteristics and capabilities of a material (or substance) make it what it is and, with regard to water, it is one of the worldly materials that exemplify transformational abilities (Ball 2002). In consequence, the way in which water is structured determines its behaviours, which in turn regulate how it can have relationships with other materials – including the amalgam of materials held together as human (and other) bodies (Barad 2003, 2007; Vokes 2013).

Giving attention to materials generally allows us to rekindle our focus on the world of which we are a part. One could argue that this is exactly what traditional scholarship has done – worked with the materials of the world to find out how they behave – and, while this is uncontestable, the realization that people are material still lies very far from our everyday, rational grasp. The NM approach differs in that it expands what constitutes 'material' to include the materiality of the human and the body in its sights. In addition, through recognition that existence is composed of interacting materials, the human (as a) body is drawn in as a set of interacting materials in a world of only materials. Thus, rather than framing materials as resources for harnessing and use by people, it accepts that all activity (including human activity) is a material arrangement that is circumscribed by virtue of the physical laws that determine behaviours and outcomes. This move, which is more concerned with substances and less interested in objects, recognizes the vitality of materials (Bennett 2010) and demonstrates the manners in which earthly substances provoke human behaviours. Therefore, it is quite distinct from past materially focused approaches, because its epistemological core encourages a rediscovery of the whole world, and everything that is part of it, as one of materials – but not just as materials, and rather as *materials in relationship with each other*.

This uncompromising, boundary blurring, material grounding promotes an alternative ethic and concomitant sensitivity to the material world and, in consequence, attempts to dethrone the human from its current place of agential authority. This highly political position reminds us of our dependencies and the need to reconsider our methods of engagement and representation. This perspective, therefore, recognizes that relationships are predicated on how materials behave and, through this recognition, hopes to contribute to an ethically rooted analytic that rejects past positions and supports the visualization of the creativity of the world through this lens.

Focusing on the connections between the materiality of water and ontologies explains how both conceptions and relationships are predicated on the way in which engaging materials are able to behave together. However, in recognition that depictions cannot successfully focus on the fundamentality (even molecularity) of engaging materials exclusively and without reference to objects, the chapters that follow show that water's behaviour cannot be uncoupled successfully from the chemistry of bodies (human or otherwise), because actions produce and are part of the wider network of relationships. Therefore, this approach reveals that everything behaves together, which, in consequence, informs cultural norms and expectations, and governs how all parties are partners and have affectively (and effectively) co-produced the manners in which they can engage with each other. Thus, this is not about using water to think with; rather, it is an approach that recognizes that water thinks (*with*) us, and that the process is not one using the other, or that it is a one-way process, but, in keeping with inherent molecular behaviours, asserts that being is a cyclic, relational activity.

My hope is that this relational methodology sutures the representational rupture that tends to occur around thinking and being. The mental detachment between the idea of materials and what they cohere into is a very well-entrenched habit of perception – so much so that it can initially feel uncomfortable to think otherwise. However, clearly, nothing exists in isolation and everything depends on there being other things to regulate and sustain the conditions favourable for life (Capra 2002), so it should not take too much to persuade oneself to move away from traditional representations towards something that recognizes process, dynamics and networks rather than individuals, items and separation. Furthermore, any tendency to imagine that thought or meaning making lies outside 'the material' needs to be interrogated seriously. As Capra so eloquently reminds us, 'cognition ... is not a representation of an independently existing world, but rather a continual bringing forth of a world through the process of living' (2002: 32), and to underline this theme further he goes on to use the example of sensation and taste to make his point. Rather, as we have already discovered, wetness is not a property of water, so Capra states that it is foolish to assume that sweetness is a property of sugar when it is the result of the sensory experience relationship that we have with it. Sweetness therefore is an occurrence and 'emergent phenomen[on]' (Capra 2002: 36), which, without our experiencing it, would not exist as it does. Therefore 'the world that we see ... is not *the* world but *a* world, which we bring forth with others' (Capra 2002: 47, citing Maturane and Varele 1987 (original emphasis)).

In recognition that water has a unique set of abilities that make its ubiquitous presence paradoxically mundane, mysterious, vital and dangerous, this approach demonstrates how the qualities of a physical material, when engaging with other materials, determine how meanings about it emerge and are enacted. Moreover, as materials 'flow, mix and mutate' (Ingold 2011: 30) together, their properties cause experiences that both tell stories and provoke conclusions about 'who' they are. A relational approach persuades one to recognize that existence is a process that uses a non-linear dynamic (Capra 2002: 12) to produce both the drastic complexity and order that we are used to, and reminds us that life is not composed of static and fixed entities but is ruthlessly and inexorably emergent and centred on the simultaneous unpredictable recycling of each other *together*. Moreover, this approach helps one to realize that behaviours are triggered because of relationships and do not exist in a vacuum but rather emerge within the possibilities inherent in any given situation. Material, therefore, is behaviour, and behaviour is always material – and the mechanisms that enact them are complicated responses that emerge with extraordinary sophistication and variety because of the manners in which interactions occur.

Latour's Actor Network Theory (ANT) contends that, as processes rely on a network of influences acting on each other (1993a), entities other than human can be attributed with agency since they act on human lives. To a degree, this notion confronts human exceptionalism by drawing in 'things' as actors on the stage of life. Similarly, by bringing forces other than human into focus, the more-than-human move recognizes existence as being produced through a co-creative ecological focus (Boivin 2008; Whatmore 2002). Both approaches challenge representation and aim to level the representational playing field (Witmore 2014) through contestation of the assumption that human activity is acting upon, and is therefore in some way divorced from, the material world (Ingold 2000, 2007). These ideas, cohering under the heading 'New Materialities', present a posthuman challenge to the vapid ideals of postmodernism (Barad 2003; Kohn 2015). They offer a call to draw the material world back into focus. This time, not just as one that is full of useful resources that coincidentally and serendipitously exist for our use, but as a realm of co-generative entities that work together to shape, resist and organize (Latour 2004). This lens gives credit to the part that materials play in making humans what they are (Ingold and Palsson 2013), and needs to be recognized overtly if future developments are to be genuinely sustainable at all levels.

The role of water in shaping human lives is both physically and culturally inescapable, as many interdisciplinary texts testify (e.g. Ball 2002; Carey 2010; Fishman 2011; Gleick 2014a and b; Lansing 1987;

Strang 2004, 2009, 2010, 2015; Wagner 2015). However, demonstration of the material agential abilities of water to provoke behaviour is only now being approached by scholarship (see paragraph below for examples). Drawing water into the foreground, as I do here, contributes to this call. The NM perspective moves past recognizing that life needs water, in favour of approaching it as a co-constituent of bodies, or as a partner that is corporeally engaged in the process of being/becoming human (Ingold 2000). Adopting this perspective allows water to be one of many characters involved in people's lives and thereby elucidates how its behaviour – what it does, where it flows – is not only relevant to ensuring a regular supply but also directly shapes people both physically and culturally. In doing so, the NM establishes that the material 'water' acts with other materials (in this case, people) to co-produce the forms that their relationships can adopt. Therefore, the ability of static water to bring misfortune if it is not allowed to move is responsible for the way in which the Giriama live with water, and the fact that ice melts in the heat of the summer prompts the Andalusians to have a water festival. Thus, I intend to demonstrate that it is not just that water is, or that it is necessary for life, but how water behaves that is accountable, formative and demands attention. Consequently, it is not just that people need water that creates practices, but rather how water behaves *with* people that determines how those practices can be enacted. This attention shift towards materials is political: it reminds us that it is not just the need for water that shapes culture in multiple ways (as the literature amply demonstrates), but it is how water behaves in different ecological and environmental settings that is responsible for the ways in which people can think about water and organize their sociality with it.

This perspective is quite different from the traditional materialist focus of scholars such as Harris (1979) or one that recognizes the influences of material culture (cf. Miller 2005). Approaching the world using an NM focus brings the physics of interaction to the fore. By looking specifically at relationships and noting how it is possible for items to engage, it reveals that, at all scales, associations are determined by the manner in which substances can interact. Thus, at the level of substances we can do away with networks that tie 'things' together in affective bondage, in favour of an intersecting, impacting complexity of influences within a field of materials in which things become what they are because of how they can come together in that moment and place. This perspective forces thinking to dissolve the intellectually imposed barriers or borders around objects and shrinks the distance between objects so that the cognitive representations of materiality chime with the world's physicality. This is not to create a bland, homogenous blanket of materials that are devoid of individuals but rather to promote a new language and thinking about the world that realizes that the perpetuation of any notion of separation is materially false, damaging and unsustainable. The NM spotlights how we are materials on a continuum with other materials becoming together. Thus, this book builds on the scholarship that aims to reassert the significance of the material world, as it were, anthropologically and ontologically (Barad 2003; Bennett 2010; Coole and Frost 2010; Ingold 2000; Kohn 2015). This is achieved not only through demonstration of how water plays a part in the articulation, mobilization and generation of bodies (individual, social and political), but through recognition that being human emerges as a relationship that is predicted by the way in which materials (in this case, water) can behave. Therefore the substances that form life should also be represented as co-productive organizing forces that act on how lives are lived, rather than simply resources to be consumed, or substances to think [with] (cf. Levi Strauss 1964). In so doing, it firmly places the human into a world of materials, thereby reminding us that, due to our own physicality, it is imperative that we recognize that we are materials working with materials (Merleau-Ponty 1968; Serres 1992). Furthermore, noting that substances shape social practices problematizes the boundaries established between what is natural and raw with what is cultural and social (Drazin and Küchler 2015). By shining a critical light on the manners in which humans currently engage with planetary substances, we have the opportunity to contribute to a deeply ethical, alternative perspective that embraces the notion of co-productivity with both hands.

This realization is producing a wide-ranging body of literature that centres materials as instrumentally active in rousing behaviours and thus informing how lives can be lived. With regard to water specifically, some remarkable examples of this are already available. For example, Chen et al.'s rich interdisciplinary text *Thinking with Water* aims to 'bring water forward for conscious and careful consideration'

(2013: 3); Helmreich's *Alien Ocean: Anthropological Voyages in Microbial Seas* (2009) approaches water anthropologically, to reveal the life of planetary water through the lens of marine microbiology; and Mathur and Da Cunha's edited collection *Design in the Terrain of Water* (2014) thoroughly problematizes conventional representations of water through their calls for 'regenerative rethinking' into how water shapes lives (2014: viii). (See also Bear and Eden 2011; Castaing-Taylor and Paravel 2012; Lahiri-Dutt 2014.) Strang's rich contribution to this area demonstrates how water troublingly flows between cultural and natural with the potential to cause both order and disorder effortlessly (see Strang 2004, 2009, 2010, 2013a and b, 2014, 2015, 2016). By adopting an NM framework, this book builds on this body of work and aims to propel discussions regarding planetary water in a materially, culturally sensitive and ethically attentive manner that realizes that current global problems are not 'exclusively human' ones (Kohn 2015: 311). In so doing, this perspective accepts and honours the affective position that materials can claim, and realizes how communities are permanently in profound conversation with their ecological partners (Boivin 2008; Cruz 2014; Malafouris 2013).

The perspective advocated here is an inclusive and phenomenological one. Moreover, it is also an honest one. Prior to our holding the knowledge of our universe that we do currently, we could have been forgiven for thinking that objects existed discretely from each other. Now, as we realize that the world blends itself into being, recognition of the materiality of existence needs to be genuinely embraced – not just knowing how to use the materials of the world, but knowing-with and learning from the materials of the world of which we are part of. This perspective hopes that, by looking past appearances and into matters, an appreciation and realization of the fundamental chemical interdependencies that tangle everything together will infuse practice and eventually counter the prevailing tides that continue to present people as consumers of the world. In association, by removing the intellectual methods that separate people from materials, it will be possible to contribute to the construction of methods that stimulate a holistic sustainable future (Barad 2003, 2007; Capra 2002; Coole and Frost 2010).

PART TWO

4 INTRODUCTION

This section offers three ethnographic examples of water relationships as appreciated through a New Materialities (NM) lens. The ethnographic information used in the chapters that follow was collected from various periods of anthropological fieldwork using mixed methods, including brief surveys, organized community meetings and meetings with local officials and stakeholders, but was obtained qualitatively, primarily through informal, spontaneous discussions and immersive participant observation.

Chapter 5 relates to a group of Giriama in rural Kenya who regularly negotiate drought and whose lives are shaped by a dearth of water as a result. It shows that being Giriama is indivisibly entangled with the way in which water behaves in the arid region that they inhabit. This results in part from continuously having to seek it, which has a significant impact on the body and on daily practices, but also arises through the multiple personal and cultural methods devised to attract and retain it, and the watery restrictions and idioms that flow through Giriama thinking. The intention of the chapter is to highlight how water's actions in this region – that is, what water does and how people are forced to relate to it – are instrumental in the co-production and moulding of daily practices and social institutions alike. From collection, to rituals, to social status and organization, water's influence is obvious. Therefore, despite – or perhaps because of – its absence, water is shown to have soaked into and pervaded social and cultural life, thereby shaping the way that people can live their lives. Consequently, in contrast to more traditional approaches that perhaps could imagine this concerns a symbolic influence or association with water, this chapter illustrates that it is the brute material connections and correspondences that form relationships and inform the physical manifestations of social and cultural life. This is not about imagining, or creating a symbolic ideation of water, nor is it a way to translate water into a medium to understand; rather, it is a physical and phenomenological association produced by 'dwelling' (Ingold 2000) with water's abilities that has shaped both practice and, correspondingly, Giriama notions of their authentic identity.

I have returned to Kenya regularly since my first visit to this community in 2009. My time in the field has varied depending on other commitments, from a few weeks initially to longer periods of some months living in the village. Each visit has focused my attention around water but from a series of different perspectives, which has afforded me a multifaceted comprehension of how water insecurities inform people's lives in this area.

Chapter 6 considers the relationships and intersections between water, people and the landscape in southern Spain, to demonstrate how water is drawn into people's lives in this area. The information in this chapter comes from my experience of Lanjaron, a rural village in mountainous Andalusia, where, in the 1990s, I purchased a small, dilapidated *cortico* (shepherd's house) that I visited regularly until 2007. Because rural homes here do not benefit from running water as urban homes do, each house and portion of land in this region is sold with an allocation of water rights, represented by a number of hours during which water can flow through a complicated series of irrigation channels onto one's fields and into one's home. The channels, constructed originally by the Moors, persuade and allow the mountain spring water or snow melt that would otherwise simply serve one area to spread across the mountainside by being directed into each property for the time specified on the deeds. This could be for as little as 15 minutes a week, and represents an important time for the occupants to ready themselves to receive and contain the water that they have been allowed. It is this method of engaging with water, and the regular discussions about water feuds between families or neighbours, that might have originally steered my attention towards the role that water plays in generating the ways that people can live.

The water in this area is considered to be health promoting because of its distinct and varied mineral content. Consequently, structures that ascertain, distribute and encourage its consumption have been constructed in the town and across Spain. Therefore, not only has the combination of the different types of waters and the seasonal scarcities in this region impelled people to offer time and energy to redirect and share water across the mountain and further abroad; they have had their lives organized by water as a result. Moreover, the significance attributed to this water arises as a result of the consequences emergent from ingestion of the water (Attala 2017: see the Edibility Approach). Therefore, water's materiality has spread its influence both in the landscape and into the bodies of the people who engage with it.

In addition, Chapter 6 illustrates how the ability of water to slow down its own movement during portions of the calendar, and to pick up minerals in solution, is responsible for the manner in which people order their relationships with it. This is evident in the structures created around each household's access to a supply, and around the annual cultural ritual behaviours and meanings associated with these waters. This section offers another example of how water shapes the way in which people can relate to it: not simply to draw it closer into their homes by coaxing it across the landscape through a maze of pathways, but also through organizing weekly points of engagement, the construction of mechanisms to retain it temporarily, and the generation of outlets and rituals that honour its 'personal' abilities.

The last ethnographic chapter of this second part of the book (Chapter 7) considers the role that water has played in shaping the modern Welsh national identity through its ability to flood, collect and amass in depressions and then be redirected out of the area in which it has collected. It takes as its starting point the trope of Wales as a wet country, which is blessed with plenty of rain and the rolling green hills that a plentiful supply of water can produce. It illustrates the ubiquity and constant presence of water in Welsh lives, and then changes direction to explore how water in quantity acts on the lives of the people who imagine that they can contain it for use. By exploring how people live with flooding and the enormous weight of contained water, this chapter makes connections between ideations of water, national identity and the materiality of watery behaviours.

5 THE GIRIAMA IN KENYA
Living with Drought

> Looking for water is Giriama. We do other things – children, goats, maize – but looking for water is being Giriama.
>
> (Kasungu Mare 2017 (pers. comm.))

I may be making assumptions, but I think it is fair to say that the majority of readers of this book will be people who access water directly in their homes through some kind of municipal system that, in exchange for a price, ensures that the water that comes into their homes is safe and constant. The overarching purpose of this chapter is to explore the part that water plays in shaping lives where water is periodically – or regularly – scarce. In such conditions, individuals are compelled to make every effort to draw sufficient supplies of water into their lives and, concomitantly, relationships with water have a tendency to dominate imaginations and thereby shape lived experience (Derman et al. 2007; Moran 2008). Consequently, water not only shapes daily routines – and people's bodies, as a result – but also impacts on the way in which people think about their lives. Moreover, this example illustrates that what water does articulates the way in which people understand how to relate to each other. Finally, a reliance on earth systems situates provision as dependent on other-than-human agencies (Descola 2013), which means that individuals must engage with those agencies to ensure supply.

In this chapter we look at how water actively participates in the lives of a group of people living in a semi-arid rural landscape of coastal Kenya. The people we are about to meet are the Giriama. They are subsistence horticultural pastoralists, which means that they cultivate gardens, herd livestock and rely directly on earth systems (rather than technology or infrastructure) to subsist. The Giriama claim that they migrated into this area from further north approximately 400 years ago (Parkin 1991). However, despite intense interdisciplinary speculation, their exact point of origin remains elusive, as extensive searches have failed to establish where they hail from successfully. Nevertheless, the Giriama are established as one of the group locally known as the Mijikenda – a collective term for the nine tribes that make claim to the area and that mainly inhabit a north-eastern coastal strip spanning from Mombasa to Lamu. There are numerous ethnic groups in Kenya. Sources cite over forty (Drabu 2017) but the exact number is unclear. The Giriama constitute 2 per cent of the total population, making them a significant minority. This chapter will relate to how the identity of a group of Giriama who live between the towns of Garashi and Marafa (in an outlying area named Boré Koromi) present their identity and connection to the land they now live with as being linked to water's behaviours, such as its ability to move, migrate to other areas, and seasonally 'hide'.

The population depends for its water supply upon a seasonal river (the Koromi) that dissects the landscape at certain times of year. A seasonal river relies on rains falling heavily in the up-country watershed to fill it, and, while all rivers rely on precipitation (rain) and groundwater to flow, the difference between a seasonal and a non-seasonal river is that a seasonal river's flow is temporary and is expected to dry up in association with the weather patterns further up its path. If the rains come in the uplands with enough force, the Koromi River will fill, and the land further downstream will feel the benefit of that water, even if rains have not fallen in that area. This is because the water will gather into what is called a watershed (a huge basin that collects rain run-off) until it reaches an overflow point from where it floods down through the pre-carved pathway or valley. The origin of seasonal rivers is notoriously difficult to locate, but locals say that the Koromi is fed from the desert upland streams such as the Bulfaji stream and the Midu waterhole that lie north-east of the Lali Hills. Both sources sit at an elevation of between 110 and 140 metres above sea level and are approximately 20–35 kilometres away from Boré.

There is water under almost all of the land. In fact, there is much more water under the earth than above it. Water under the ground is called 'ground water' and its level is called the 'water table'. Below the water table is the level at which the ground is saturated with water.

Areas in which water pockets under the land are called 'aquifers'. The water table forms through a process of infiltration whereby water saturates the ground, while also filling the underground aquifers. The water table creates both a buffer (to stop leakage) and a recharge source of water for rivers as they meander down and back to the sea. Thus, the water that we see in a river is only a small amount of the total body of water present in that area. Under the ground (and horizontally to the sides) of rivers a significant amount of water feeds it and seemingly flows with it. Ground water is chemically different from surface water because of different levels in nitrates, carbon dioxide, ammonium etc. (Ramberg et al. 2006) that 'result [from] . . . a complex interplay of climate, morphology, soils, geology, vegetation and hydrology' (Ramberg et al. 2006: 678) of a location.

In this part of Kenya the water accumulated in the uplands flows down towards the sea, filling any of the depressions or basins of the Koromi pathway that it encounters on its journey. It is the numerous, scattered and variable basins on which the population fundamentally relies for its domestic water supply, using it for livestock and other domestic needs such as drinking, cooking and washing. We should remember that a seasonal river is, by definition, periodic and episodic. This means that it does not flow as a perennial river does: it is semi-permanent and ephemeral, reliant on rains falling in another location as well as locally, and, most importantly, has a tendency regularly to run dry if the necessary meteorological conditions are not met. Seasonal rivers can rely on multiple sources for their water. In the case of the River Koromi, when the upland sources receive enough rainfall, the river bed (and therefore the basins) will fill, producing a temporary dark shimmering snake of water across the landscape – until the flow subsides and the landscape is left with trapped water in what amounts to very large, deep puddles.

As a result of the climate and the intense heat that bakes down throughout the year in this area, rain and the notion of 'the rains' describe a quite different climatic activity to the rain that one might expect to experience in other locations. When people talk of 'the rains' in Boré Koromi, they are referring to a very specific type of penetrating downpour that soaks down into the sandy ground by a distance of a few feet. 'The rains', then, mean more than a shower or two – or even constant rain. The phrase 'the rains' describes enough water to cause a flood – so much water that it can seep down into the ground before the surrounding air temperature forces it to rise again through the process of evapo-transpiration. Thus, there are many days on which, strictly speaking, it rains – but not enough to be considered of any consequence or significance. On those days, people will deny that it has rained. 'That's not rain', they say. 'Rain is when you can dig down afterwards and find puddles of water soaked into the ground.'

The north-eastern section of Africa has a history replete with periods of intense, life-threatening drought, and has inevitably suffered recurring conflict as a result. Indeed, drought is so common for the people in the Horn of Africa that they have created numerous mechanisms to cope with it (Moran 2008). When one's existential security or ability to survive is directly connected to one's ability to regularly access water, an awareness of water and a plethora of practices that draw it into one's life shapes one's thinking and orders daily activities. As a result, Giriama life is inundated with water practices, regulations and taboos.

Water practices: rain, roofs, rivers and water basins

Obviously, river water is not the only water that flows into Giriama lives. It comes from a variety of other sources: wells, water pans and the rains that periodically fall across the fields. In conjunction, water is considered in multiple and not singular terms. Indeed, the word 'water' in Giriama (pronounced *maadzi*) recognizes its ability to be something while also being multiple things. This makes water a collective noun that is able to be simultaneously one and many. As a result, each type of water has its own methodologies and taboos associated with it. These methods ensure that activities are effective because they maintain order with regard to each kind of water. Water's capability – that is, its ability to be one and many – proves to be of fundamental significance not only to daily practice but also to Giriama identity.

Head carrying: water shaping gendered bodies

Water must be collected on a daily basis, and, depending on the size of one's family, the journey to the water source may need to be completed a few times each day. Collecting water is considered to be women's work. Literature shows that 'domestic load-carrying, as a low-status activity, is regarded culturally as a "female" activity in most African societies . . . The burden, in time and effort, thus falls disproportionately on women and children' (Porter et al. 2013: 90). This is quite assertively stated by men and recalcitrantly acknowledged by women.

Musa, a middle-aged farmer living with his wife and ten small children, explains that the ancestors established water collection as women's work because 'they thought that the women were lower than us' (2016, pers. comm.). This conception emerges in association with the fact that women are bought into households through a bridewealth payment system, from which men then assume the role of owner and their wives that of property. This practice is deeply rooted in the past, where women, power and wealth were perhaps more obviously socially intertwined. For example, Cashmore (1961) claims that women were bought and sold as slaves among the Giriama, and even used as collateral in times of economic stress. Despite changes in practice with regard to overt slavery, the purchase of women remains not only an organizing principle of gender relations for the Giriama, but is also driven and enmeshed by water. When prompted to consider what might happen if people did not pay for their wives, the question of who would collect water was raised.

> Oh! That's difficult, because no one would have the power over the other! It is a shame for the man to collect water.
> (Musa 2016, pers. comm.) ['It is a shame' translates as this brings shame on him.]

Buying women is formalized through the marriage ceremony, after which the phrase '*Umepata jiko*' (trans. 'You have got a kitchen') is used to describe the relationship. As the phrase suggests, women are expected to make the man's life easier by taking over most of the daily activities that life demands, such as collecting water.

However, to claim that water collection is the sole domain of women is inaccurate. Unmarried men and boys carry their own water until they have the benefit of a 'kitchen'. There are, however, restrictions on how to carry the water. Males must not use their heads for the task, and are expected to use their backs, donkeys or bicycles instead. Women jokingly claim that men do not have the right head shape for the task.

To bring water to the household, women usually wake and start their journey to the nearest river basin before first light each day. The walk to the water can be achieved relatively quickly without a load but it can still take some of the women in this area over an hour to get to the water, depending on where they live. The aim is to bring water back for breakfast and washing before the sun gets too hot or the children are awake. Thus, leaving at around 5 a.m. to collect water is normal for many women.

Women can carry only one 20-litre jerry can per trip but, as a family needs a lot more water per day, after breakfast and after setting the washed children off to school, women must return to the water source to get more. The number of trips depends on family size. The average is four round trips per day – equating, for some, to over four hours, often with a baby either strapped to one's back or *in utero* (Porter et al. 2013). As the last trip of the day is done with the children (after their return from school), more than 20 litres can be collected in that final evening journey. With water collection occurring when the day is at its coolest, women are free to work in their gardens (*shambas*) and complete other tasks, such as collecting firewood, making charcoal, washing, construction and preparing food, in the heat of the day.

The time spent carrying water acts on and shapes women's lives, as much as the weight of the water that they carry shapes their bodies. For some, this means that they can do little else in the day. Furthermore, as nearly all activities demand water, women's bodies reflect the relationships that they have with water. In contrast to the few Kambe women in the area who can carry water by strapping it on to their backs, Giriama women must carry the water that they collect on their heads. Both methods leave women's hands free – a technique that is not only useful for those with small children but also allows water collection journeys to double up for other purposes. The body strength needed to carry 20 litres of water by hand for even a five-minute walk causes immense strain and effort. On the head, however, it is an entirely different matter. Carrying water (and other heavy items) on the head centres the weight of the object down through the centre of the body rather than allowing it to draw the carrier to one side or the other (Heglund et al, 1995), twisting the spine and adding strain. Furthermore, research shows that 70 per cent of a person's body weight can be moved by using the head with only a small amount of extra exertion, if the person has been trained (Lloyd et al. 2010), which offers a convincing explanation for head carrying when other automated mechanisms of transportation are not available.

Despite the above, collecting water is undoubtedly arduous. Women talk of their legs hurting so much on some days that they cannot bear to walk any more. Women in other studies also complain of neck pain each day after collecting water (Geere et al. 2010a and b). Lifting 20 litres (equal to 20 kilogrammes) up and on to one's head is beyond most people on their own. Lifting the water from ground level is difficult enough. Men and women similarly strain to shift a full jerry can from the tap after it has been filled. They wrench the can away from the faucet and let it fall to the ground with a thump. They can do little else, as it is so heavy – their bodies are pulled by the weight of the water sloshing around in the can. Each woman helps the other. Even nearby women who are not collecting will get up to help someone with their water. Thus, once the jerry can is filled, assistance is needed to help raise the dense weight above head height. For this, the women must work together: the individual who is to carry the water first takes a scarf and coils it into a circular 'nest', which she then places on her head. Then, retaining a level head so as to not drop the coiled scarf from its position, she brings the container up as far as she can alone. She does this while slightly bending at the knees, to reduce her height. This is when her companion steps in. Both heave – getting the can to waist level, together. Taking some of the weight of the water container in both arms, one helps the other woman, who will carry the water, to lift it up on to her now lowered, but not tipped, head. Then, in one last heave, the container is pushed up to above head height together – with one woman taking most of the weight in the final moments, the woman who is to carry the can is served with the container on her head. Once raised, the carrier stands taller, taking the full weight of the water, which settles on to her head, cushioned by the scarf's coils. Using micro-neck muscle movements to keep the water steady, she now has to help her companion to do the same – except that now she also has to keep her own water container on her head at the same time.

Once on the head, the groaning weight of the water alters and miraculously appears to lessen. Now the woman looks able to carry the container gracefully and almost without effort. The weight of the water – now seemingly insubstantial – is buoyantly maintained even while she picks up small children or other items that she will take on her journey. Heglund et al. (1995) attribute this to the pendulum-like gait maintained by the relationship between body and water, the swing of which 'maintain[s] the motion of a common centre of the body and load' (1995: 52). Indeed, watching and walking with women shows the steady flow of the body from the head down as they propel forwards while balancing the water on their heads. The load is physically unstable because of how water behaves and, according to Beaucave-Gauvreau et al. (2011), walking increases load instability. From experimentation, Beaucave-Gauvreau et al. (2011) show that women must compensate by minimizing upper body movement while moving forwards. As a result, they are obliged to use the neck and upper body to steady the bobbing contents. Water in Africa makes the rural population of women suffer from time poverty, but it has also been shown to affect their health detrimentally (Geere et al. 2010a). Constant posture modification is thought to produce degenerative changes in the neck and spine (Echarri and Forriol, 2005). However, Beaucave-Gauvreau et al. (2011) concede that load carrying may also be beneficial for bone density.

As can be seen from the above, women's subjugation is culturally and materially entangled with the need to collect water. Carrying water itself, coupled with the distances covered, means that women are shackled to the process. Furthermore, any system that prevents women from having to walk and collect water implies that their time could be freed up – something that, while desirable, does not seem to be suitable to some of the community. When women are asked to imagine a life without water collection being a part of it, they are unable to imagine themselves in alternative occupations, having no frame of reference on which to draw. Equally, men are verbal about the need for women to be occupied with tasks for the home, as they do not want them to stray.

In association with the relentless search for water and the backbreaking work that is needed to bring adequate amounts to the homestead, Kasunga, an elderly member of the community, claims that 'looking for water *is* Giriama'. He is not translating the word, but is acknowledging the unremitting search for water that being Giriama in this region demands. This is also not simply because life cannot survive without water but because it is in the water that the identity of the Giriama is both materially and culturally suspended.

Giriama conceptions of water

Giriama cosmology understands water materially – that is, in terms of its physical behaviours and what it can do. Relationships with water are, first and foremost, quotidian and pragmatic, but, equally, they are personally complex and cosmologically troubled. For example, as the Giriama hold that water is attractive to other-than-human entities that can cause harm, practices that encourage it to be held stationary for any length of time are cautioned against, in a bid to avoid its tendency to become dangerous.

'Giriama believed water to be life still they believed that stagnant water was shelter to demons' (verbatim transcript from email correspondence, Alex Katana Mare 2015). That demons 'shelter' in and around water is a common belief, but it is also contested knowledge; nevertheless, the daily requirement for the fluid must supersede anyone's concerns. Consequently, collecting, retaining and drinking the river water are equally mundane and dangerous activities.

This community has always relied on environmental conditions and ritual sacrifice to provide the community water as rain. Community members agree that, until very recently, traditional rainmaking rituals have been a consistent and reliable method of acquiring water in Giriama life. Rain brings water to the community, falling without judgment or prejudice on all community members simultaneously. How water behaves as rain, therefore, is of political significance as it does not favour or single out individuals for privileged treatment but shares its influence with an amount of equity.

Fu ha mwenga: fluidity and identity

> Brothers cannot go hungry if you have food in your house.
> (Agnes Ngumbao 2016 (pers. comm.))

The Giriama of Boré regularly use the phrase '*fu ha mwenga*', which translates as either 'We are together' or literally as 'We are one'. This phrase regularly punctuates dialogue to indicate that the engaging parties recognize their connection and that, because they are connected therefore automatically have an obligation to support each other.

Determining whether 'We are together' sits at the core of social relationships. How one is together with another (or with the group) impacts on all relationships – human and otherwise. Indeed, it can be held as the articulating idea that places the Giriama as dwelling with the world (and each other), rather than on it (Ingold 2000).

The process of establishing similarity (and togetherness) through kin and alliance networks is an obvious mechanism that is used by all cultures in different ways. Establishing similarity with strangers, on the other hand, offers particular problems and can take a long time to complete. When an individual meets another with whom they are not familiar – for example, on the road – he or she must begin the process of finding out just how much the other is 'together' with them. This is done through a complicated series of elaborate and structured questions that reveal information about clan (*mbari*), family (*mviago*), location and heritage or ancestry. These questions are initially asked with a sense of suspicion – something akin to mistrust and certainly trepidation. Faces are slightly turned away, bodies positioned side on to each other and eye contact is avoided. The bevy of questions that follows is designed to reveal just how close the other person is to you – if you are family, if you are '*mwenga*' (trans: 'one'). Once this is determined one is able to understand the immediate obligations of the relationship, as will the other person. This then sets the stage for future behaviours and shapes the level of culturally expected engagement.

If the interchange manages to establish even the slightest link – and they usually do – then everyone visibly relaxes, as one is considered, even named as, part of the wider family group within one of the seven Giriama clans. To be positioned as part of the family in this manner dissolves attention on one's individuality and foregrounds the place that one takes in the wider network of expectations that draw the Giriama together. Networks, of course, do not represent one-way streets but rely on the efficacy of the links to maintain the structure and ensure that all involved uphold the bonds. Thus, in tandem with this, the process of establishing that, *fu ha mwenga* (we are together) acts to reinforce the wider web of associates, our place in the network and affirms the idea that we should not consider ourselves as being alone, or having to fend for ourselves without support.

However, with non-Giriama this can be more difficult, and so there is a mechanism to draw strangers into the family group by naming them. Thus, the family connection can be completely independent of any notion of bloodlines, alliances or ethnic similarity. Willis and Miers (1997), demonstrate the fluidity and significance of kin membership in Giriama society in their discussion of how to understand the incorporation of others into Giriama families.

> In the early nineteenth century there was a steady intake of 'outsiders' into Giryama society. Giryama was a permeable identity, its permeability premised on the incorporative dynamics of an economy which sought to invest surplus in human relationships. Claims on people were the basis of wealth, and of security in times of conflict or difficulty. Whenever they could, people acquired more such claims.
>
> The circumstances of these 'outsiders' varied considerably. Some were men and women driven by a desire to improve their circumstances. One man summarized the motives of his migrant ancestor quite simply, 'He was seeking wealth'. Others were individuals or small family groups driven by the local shortages made commonplace by the fickle rains of the coast. Others still came fleeing disputes, illness or witchcraft which threatened their security. Some came as brides in return for bridewealth. Others were offered by their kin as security for loans or as compensation for the offences of their elders. Some were captured in warfare. A few – but probably quite a few, in the early nineteenth century – were bought from coastal or other traders in return for commodities.
>
> (Willis and Miers 1997: 483)

Kinship therefore does not rely on connections produced by marriage or birth, as even those individuals bought into families became 'brothers and sisters' (Willis and Miers 1997: 480).

In addition, for example, I am now family, and my Giriama name (*Kadzo*) reflects that. (*Kadzo* can mean someone who has everything or beauty.) Being named is hailed as both a privilege and an honour, and furthermore allows one safe passage across the district. Misfortunes can be attributed to a stranger's entry into a space, if they are not recognized as a member of the group. Thus, prior to my acceptance as family, I was chaperoned everywhere. This was deemed vital for both my protection and that of the wider group. Being accompanied ensured that misfortune did not befall anyone. Even now, as family, there are places that I cannot go alone because it would be hard to explain my difference.

My naming was delivered with whoops of delight and generalized merriment, with women loudly ululating in appreciation of what, at the time, I thought to be the recognition of our mutual similarity and connection. However, I was mistaken. In my case, being part of a family and a clan comes not with an acknowledgement of likeness but with a tie that binds one to what feels like a weighty obligation to support my family. With the obvious power inequalities between the local population and myself, its obtaining me as family implies a lifeline to economic security. Therefore, the group strategically named me in accordance with what the community collectively recognized that I could give to it – and not, as I initially assumed, in recognition of being personally accepted. Having taken the name, I am now family, which means that I can be (and am regularly) called on to help my family when they think that they need it. Equally, the obligation is reciprocal, and I, too, can call on them for information without resentment.

> Water is many, so it is like one as many. *Fu ha mwenga* applies here.
> (Stephen Ngumbao 2017 (pers. comm.))

Greeting practices and absorbing or dissolving the difference of visitors are clearly illustrative of the cultural force that *fu ha mwenga* exerts and mirrors the manner by which water manifests and is understood. Greetings with the Giriama are highly structured, regardless of familiarity. For people that one sees regularly, including close family, each encounter must be opened with a series of phrases that are sometimes all but muttered at each other. Entry into a populated space requires one to greet every person in turn, using a similar volley of expressions for each. Hands are held, slapped or touched, depending on status; similarly, the level of audibility and whether to hold eye contact or look to the ground depends on one's position in the social hierarchy.

Women tend to look away from men while reciting the greetings – as do children, who also offer limp hands to touch. Different phrases are used for different age groups. Elders or individuals with status must be met with an arm outstretched but with the other arm crossing the body, the hand resting on the outstretched arm's elbow as a measure of one's respect. Depending on the amount of people in an area, the act of greeting can consume a lot of time. Trading partners are also drawn into the system by making them part of what Zeleza called a 'blood brotherhood' (1995: 18). Blood brothers pledge an oath that draws the entire family – not just the individuals trading – into the set of obligations.

To fail to greet an individual causes social consternation. If you neglect to greet another it indicates that you do not hold them in your sights and you are not thinking about them because you are too absorbed by other thoughts. Doing this once or twice will be tolerated, but more than that will draw questions to find out what is occupying you so much that you cannot notice the people around you. Thinking about things other than those around you is mistrusted. People imagine that you might be plotting or scheming for personal gain that ignores your membership of the group.

Through the constant referral to others, each person realizes that they inhabit a place within a group. This perspective draws the focus from the self as an individual to one of the self as part of the community. Thus, when one family is in jeopardy, there is a sense that every family is, and actions are taken to support those in need, but only in reference to the whole. This communistic sense of being together is also reflected in other social practices. For example, Zeleza describes Giriama families taking turns to work each other's farmland (*kukumbana*) (1995: 47), and another example is that of the activities that depend on *harambee*. *Harambee* is a KiSwahili (not Giriama) term for 'Let's pull together' but is the label used for activities demanded of community members without payment. It is regularly invoked across Kenya and has similarities with the Bantu humanist philosophy of *Ubunte* used in South Africa, which reminds people of their interconnectedness. *Harambee*, or 'pulling together', occurs periodically at particular shared events. *Fu ha mwenga*, on the other hand, is a recurring cultural idiom that articulates social life. As a result, it is also subtler, works as a constant reminder that one lives as a dependent part of a wider whole, and as a social force it effectively liquefies the individual into the group. Therefore being regularly reminded that the group *is* together constantly lubricates Giriama social life. Indeed, as will become clear, 'being together' with water itself embodies the very essence or authenticity of Giriama-ness.

Being together is both challenging to, and threatened by, separation and difference. The potent(ial) danger of being separate and different is nowhere more clearly illustrated than in hospitality theory (Candea and de Col 2012). The ritualized actions of hospitality ameliorate the vulnerability induced by the notion of the strange(r) penetrating the social body (Derrida and Dufourmantelle 2000). Establishing whether *fu ha mwenga* (if we are together) is the first necessary action in all engagements and, as such, can be interpreted as the precursor to, or initiation of, further hospitality rituals that assimilate – or, in this case, engulf – the stranger into the group. The outcome of the elaborate set of greeting questions used by the Giriama is the categorization of the engaging parties into similar or different social bodies. This process determines how the interacting parties should continue to relate to each other. Thus, by sorting through genealogy, the notion of *fu ha mwenga* dissolves the potentially destabilizing force or poison of difference (Douglas 1966) and self-interest to materialize.

Watery identities

> Because water is where humans are made. Water is powerful because it comes from God – even if it is in the river, it comes from above. That is why the water can heal by pouring it. The water comes from above. Water represents togetherness, water is powerful because everything is made of it . . . The Mijikenda are 9 but also 1 – one but many – *fu ha mwenga*. God hears people who are gathered . . . <u>mwenga!</u>
>
> (Daniel Kalume Muvondi Nydura 2017 (pers. comm.))

All the Giriama with whom I have spoken recount the story of their ancestry similarly. They state that they originate from a place called *Singwaya* – a place that they enigmatically situate, without a clear reference point, somewhere 'in the north'. *Singwaya*, it is claimed, was a city with permanent housing, royalty and great riches, where everyone was more affluent and comfortable than they are today – a paradisiacal, flourishing, developed and wealthy kingdom of high-status individuals. Forced by constant conflict from unnamed herding neighbours who let cattle graze on Giriama crops, for safety they moved south into the then dense forest coastal strip, where they lived in fortified forest encampments for their protection and to preserve their authenticity. In keeping with other aspects of Giriama origins, there is some lack of clarity about the date of this movement into the area. For the Giriama around the Boré district, then, the tale of a fantastic location and story of previous riches offers a glimpse at, and perhaps validates, a powerful identity that, at first appearance, seems to lie in diametric opposition to the social status and lived reality that most Giriama occupy in contemporary Kenya.

For Parkin, on the other hand, *Singwaya* is very much a place, which he locates north of the Tana River in Somalia. He continues to say that it is 'a significant reference point of origin' (1991: 23) and goes on to substantiate this by explaining that Giriama burials are structured so as to include this place of origin: that is, corpses rolled on to their sides need their eyes to be facing the north, as though looking back to home. This is not a practice that I have come across. However, Parkin was working with a group of Giriama who live significantly further down the coast, near Kilifi. In contrast, my informants are clear that burial methods indicate the lack of significance of material reference points in the landscape. Headstones are rarely used, and graves are danced flat (Zeleza 1995). Any wooden carvings made of the deceased are not placed near the gravesite but sit, as a family member, in the compound. As a consequence of constant migration in the past, I was told, 'the dead understand the living must move on' (Theophrastus 2016 (pers. comm.)). Thus, over time, the dead bodies of the Giriama simply merge back into the landscape without emotion or sentimentality for the flesh, leaving little or no reference point for the living to revisit in the land. The dead, however, do have similar needs to those of the living, and therefore must be remembered through food sharing and regular communication. From this, one could conclude that land itself fails to be of the material importance that one might assume it to have. Consequently, the point of significance lies not in the claim of migration, or any links to a piece of geography, but in the details of the journey. Most texts fail to offer any description of the journey and very little on how it is thought to have ended. Further attention to the events of the journey and how it concludes reveals an alternative picture that suggests that water plays a leading role in making the Giriama material beings.

Identity solutions: blending place, power and water

> Of central interest here are the political implications of the intricate relationship between water, memory and landscape. In these senses, the variety of practices and languages associated with water often appear not so much as responses to a scarce 'natural' resource but rather as cultural and political resources in themselves; a kind of 'symbolic capital'.
>
> (Fontein 2008: 746)

Discussion reveals that water plays a quiet but key role in local narratives of the Giriama flight into Kenya. According to those with whom I have spoken, prior to departure, group leaders (elders and ritual practitioners) were concerned that the journey could dilute the purity of the group's identity in transit as a result of the new influences that they might encounter. Seemingly to avoid a scattering of people and the possibility of losing a sense of collectivity, the group leaders created a magic potion or medicine from local plants and water held in a clay pot (*nyungu*), which is called the *fingo* (Mutoro 1985).

Multiple accounts describe the *fingo* (Parkin 1991; Zeleza 1995). In some, it is a stone talisman (e.g. Parkin 1991), while in others it is simply described as a medicine (e.g. Mutoro 1985; Zeleza 1995). For the locals of Boré Koromi, the *fingo* was liquid, not stone. Its purpose was to contain, protect and preserve the essence and authenticity of Giriama-ness both in transit and on arrival (Parkin 1991). I have not found a text that offers comprehensive details of the recipes used to produce Giriama medicines, but conversations affirm that medicines typically use river water as the base, which is then mixed with other materials (such as hair, blood, leaves and ash) that together transmit the required communication and produce the necessary outcome. Brantley talks of the Giriama using 'ritual water' (1979: 126) so as to broadcast cultural messages to wider spheres. Referring to the burial of water medicines specifically, Brantley notes that water-based medicines are able to affect everyone within the radius of their influence simultaneously. The potency of water materials is of significance, as locals maintain that watery medicines accumulate strength over time (see Attala 2016a) as a result of the manner by which the materials are able to relate. Thus, the potency and agency of the medicines are due to three things: the activities of the spirits that the medicines are designed to attract (Alex Katana Mare 2015 and 2016 (pers. comm.)); the ability of practitioners to permeate items with power through making oaths or uttering into the materials that are blending (Theophrastus 2016 (pers. comm.)); and because, as the ingredients blend or dissolve into each other, the remaining liquid concentrates and intensifies (Freddy 2013 and 2016 (pers. comm.)).

Carried throughout their flight, the potent liquid also came with a terrible price. The medicine, while able to keep misfortune away, also exerted a destructive power, which endangered those who physically handled it. Consequently, transportation of the potion was an act of sacrifice: each individual who volunteered to carry the potion died at the end of the day.

> The original pot carried [a] . . . power – it was dangerous.
> (Theophrastus 2016 (pers. comm.))

> The custom was to carry it. Carrying the medicine pot protected the people. The carrier dies each night to sacrifice for the group. The pot fell and broke into pieces with a sound. It made a noise: *di-go*. Di is the noise. Go means finished. To show the past had finished. That pot, it protected the people. With no pot to carry now how were the people to keep together? So the people spread.
> (Stephen Ngumbao 2013 (pers. comm.))

> The pot was called Ngiriama. [Each] person who died, the place was named after him. The process ended with the digo. There a home was created.
> (James 2013 (pers. comm.))

This set of circumstances not only hints at the coherence for the community and the significance of the blending of individuality, but also reveals that the group's collective identity is experienced as being inextricably unified with a range of other materials, of which water is one (cf. Fontein 2015). According to the people who recounted the story to me, it was accepted, without complaint, that one had to die each day for the benefit of the group. This chain of deaths continued until the pot was dropped, smashing the container on the ground and emptying its contents into the soil. Once the group was unable to travel any further, this spot was where the new Giriama world was built. Any further travel was prohibited by this incident because the material that embodied Giriama-ness and provided cultural protection was now absorbed into the land. It was here that the first *Kaya* (fortified village/home) was built. This event – that is, the absorption of watery Giriama-ness into the ground – presumably worked to imbue the surroundings with a genuine sense of who the Giriama are and enabled a feeling of home to be created in foreign lands. This version contradicts Parkin's (1991) account that the *fingo* was buried, but supports his notion that the *fingo* acts as a bridge to Giriama origins. Consequently, the *fingo* both embodied and produced the Giriama.

It is hard to know how to use the word 'medicine'. The Giriama use it, and therefore so do I. However, modern usage of the term implies a substance that is used for healing or curing ailments, but the watery decoctions described by the Giriama are not created for such purposes exclusively. Rather than healing alone, in this case, medicines are used to evoke material changes other than those of the body, including bringing rain, love, employment and protection. The etymology of the word 'medicine' stems from the ancient Indo-European root 'mad' or 'med', as in to 'meditate', or to 'think with or about' (Charen 1951: 215), and, in concert with this, the Giriama medicines need to be thought about in order to be effective. Thus, Parkin uses the term 'oath medicine' (1991: 151) to indicate that the ingredients must be associated with words in order to work. Theophrastus substantiated this view when he explained the many ways in which we can use Giriama methods to influence change:

> To make a spell the practitioner will go to their special object and talk to their object saying what they want to happen. They will add their own words and then it will happen. If their object is a tree they will take leaves and roots and mix it with water. Or they could boil the roots and make a tea. They can take the root and leaves and burn them with other objects like snail shells, skins, snakes and

then grind the ash to be smooth, like powder and then take a knife or razor blade and after making small cuts on the joints pack the cuts with the ash. The power now acts. If you want to create harm you talk to the root and leave it on the path – underground – say the name of the person who you want to harm and the harm will come. Knowledge travels from blood to blood but it is not hereditary. It is like writing, you have to learn it.

(Theophrastus 2016 (pers. comm.))

Parkin describes the recipe for an oath used by the very powerful *Fisi* (hyena) clan, stating that 'it consists of liquid made from leaves and/ or roots and, according to accounts, kills unrepentant evildoers' (1991: 151). Those in the *Fisi* group are considered to be the peacekeepers or police of the Giriama (Parkin 1991). They are known to be very powerful. Today, many fear the oaths that the *Fisi* are capable of making. Other recipes include water that has washed the genitals of postmenopausal women from each clan (1991: 151). Citing Johnston (1976: 265), Parkin notes that medicines are inactive until they are 'orally instructed to have their effect' (1991: 176). Oaths can be consumed, buried and left to strengthen, and bind those using them together. Parkin likens this connectivity to the kinship of blood brotherhoods (1991: 180), but, from a New Materialities (NM) perspective, this can be understood as the co-generative agency produced by the engaging materials.

MaKaya: home from home

Kaya is the name used to describe the original Mijikenda settlements constructed after the infamous move of the Giriama into Kenya 400 years ago (Krijtenburg 2013; Nyamweru et al. 2008; Spear 1978). Constructed, perhaps, as a response to the violence that originally propelled them to migrate, the settlements now represent the central heart of Giriama culture, authenticity and power (Parkin 1991; see also Attala 2017). According to Krijtenburg (2013), the word *Kaya* translates as one's home (plural: *Makaya* describes both homes or towns/villages (Parkin 1991)), but, in this case, *Kaya* is used to name a particular type of hidden and sometimes barricaded structure that the Mijikenda constructed in the dense ridge of forest that used to run inland, perpendicular to the eastern coast and the Indian Ocean. The translation, therefore, is somewhat misleading, because a *Kaya* is not an individual's home but rather is a collective or community fortress, designed as a protected space for ritual, not mundane activities. Moreover, local accounts show that when the *Kaya* were in use, only ritual practitioners and elders gained access to its centre, while the bulk of the population lived around the outside of the structure, in clearings without protection from its walls. Nevertheless, the *Kaya* represent important cultural spaces of intangible heritage (UNESCO 2016).

Today, the United Nations Educational, Scientific and Cultural Organization (UNESCO) preserves these spaces as signature Giriama settlement heritage sites. Its documentation states that thirty *Kaya* centres are positioned inland and within the ridge of forest that runs parallel to the coast (UNESCO 2008, 2016). As examples of intangible heritage, justification for their protection stems from the sites' embodiment of 'metonymic significance for the Mijikenda' and because they 'are a fundamental source of Mijikenda's "being-in-the-world" . . . within the cultural landscape of contemporary Kenya' (UNESCO 2016). Kasungu Katana, an active advocate, campaigner and young Giriama from the town of Marafa, a few kilometres from Boré, has worked hard to revitalize traditional cultural spaces in the landscape. His work has contributed towards demonstrating the continued contemporary socio-political significance of the *MaKaya* for the tribes of the Mijikenda.

My personal knowledge of a *Kaya* is that of *Kaya Singwaya*, near Garashi. As with other *MaKaya*, this one is positioned in the remains of a forest. However, despite being protected, this sacred land now lies adjacent to a fairly well-used dirt road that leads to the water system located at Baricho that now feeds the area. The centre of the *Kaya* is little more than a cleared region but it still acts as the symbolic heart of a community that originally came through this location on its journey from the north. It was here, I was informed by Mr Nyoka who looks after the *Kaya*, that important community discussions between elders and significant rituals (such as those to bring rain) were enacted in secrecy and security, protected by the concealed position in the forest. To enhance the sanctuary and mystery of the setting, it is said to be impossible to enter the *MaKaya* without the assistance and agreement of the spirits who follow one's progress through the area invisibly. If taboos are transgressed or the spirits simply take a dislike to someone, they will trouble their journey and make them lost. To protect the space further, one is able to access the centre only through the two secreted access points, both of which are indicated by tiny unremarkable signs in the landscape (Attala 2017). These disguised entrance sites force access through thin, almost imperceptible (to the untrained eye) pathways that lead one in. Without knowledge of the route, it is easy to find oneself quite lost and unable to penetrate into the *Kaya*, as was the case for me on my first visit to *Kaya Singwaya*. The design and location of *MaKaya* used by the Mijikenda suggest the intentions simultaneously to deter unwanted incomers, protect cultural purity and create a safe space in which to use ritual powers without attention. Any sense of the mysterious about *MaKaya* is further amplified by claims of defensive and deadly potions consisting of magical and secret ingredients being buried or soaked into the ground on the premises.

The efficacy of any potion correlates to the materials of which it is composed. Potions have different functions: for example, the *fingo* (described earlier) was designed to embody Giriama authenticity in its material composition. Its makers utilized such strong magic that even just inadvertent disturbance, as it lay in the ground, would activate a deadly force (Parkin 1991; Wanza and Mugwima 2012), consequently deterring unsolicited guests who, on entry, might dilute the substance of Giriama authenticity. Thus, the purpose of *MaKaya* was not only to create a ritual and parliamentary seat for the community leaders but also to imbue a space with the material essence of Giriama-ness. Such places enable the health and purity of being Giriama to be maintained (Parkin 1991: 42). Today, the *MaKaya* are uninhabited and run down but are still considered important and powerful places by all of the Giriama with whom I have talked.

In addition, *MaKaya* are significant spaces for maintaining relationships with water and ensuring that they are unimpeded. Water affairs were safeguarded through regular sacrifice and rain-making rituals (Parkin 1991; Zeleza 1995). Even today, when tap water has been made available for purchase through roadside kiosks in some areas of the community, many locals continue to rely on and stress the effectiveness of the past communal ritual practices that 'called' the water to the fields. The ability to organize the rain is socially significant, as it is an activity that supports the collective rather than the individual. In contrast to the impartiality and neutrality of rain in a region, tap water articulates an individualistic message, as it is most pointedly available to only one person at a time. Consequently, the development of a system that is designed to provide water through a pipe with a tap presents as a dramatic restructuring of water relationships for a community that, until now, has relied on the rain that falls for each person simultaneously and without pecuniary price. Therefore, the rain-making rituals guarantee harvests and livelihood security for the collective, while tap water is available only if a person can pay for it.

However, drawing water into the community by using ritual practices also comes with a cost, as the entities that hold the water hidden in the larger 'cool' trees of the forest demand that a series of sacrificial negotiations takes place before it can be released (the word 'cool' references their ability to produce shade). Thus, not only is it necessary to communicate; it is also necessary to have a working relationship with the spirits if they are to be persuaded to 'bring the water from the big trees to the nearby sources of water' (Alex Katana Mare 2016 (pers. comm.)).

Giriama waters and authenticity: understanding the materiality of water

In this case, water's ability to take in, hold on to, transport, hide and carry other substances allows it to become the most effective material for the job of successfully transferring a group from one district to another safely. Thus, water is *the solution* that enabled Giriama-ness to be carried into the area, and as such not only embraces, conveys and preserves but also shares and spreads Giriama identity and power. Resonating with the notion of persons as dividuals, as used by Marriott (1976) – that is, persons as open composites in flux, from which seeping substances actively influence (Daniel 1984; Lamb 2000; Nair-Venugopal and Paramazivam 2012) – the water in this potion contains the collective in which individuality is dissolved and powers (in this case, various other forest materials – specifically, leaves) are subsumed and blended into an amorphous, shifting but coherent unit that is together, or many as one (*fu ha mwenga*). Some years after Marriott (1976), Strathern (1999) adopted the term 'dividual' to describe personhood in Melanesia (Marriott (1976) was concerned with India exclusively; since Strathern, other authors have used the term to describe personhood across Asia generally (Nair-Venugopal and Parmazivam 2012)). The concept acknowledges the materiality of bodies and the porosity of body boundaries.

To align bodies and personhood with substances – for example, water and fire (Abrams 1996; Harvey 2005; Vokes 2013), but also wood/phyto-matter (Kohn 2013; Narby 1998; Parkin 1991; Purpura 2009; Turnbull 1987) – is a recurring ethnographic premise. Analysis has typically translated these practices as being rooted in symbolism or totemic attachments. However, more recent approaches have shied away from what is considered to be the damage of translation, in favour of posthuman methodologies and analyses that allow multiple perspectives or ontologies (Descola 2013; Kohn 2015) to exist simultaneously – as though alongside or in relationship with each other. Using this approach, ideas do not have to make sense or be sensible, but rather will *make one able to sense* (Attala 2016b) the world of another. In conjunction, an NM perspective rejects the notion that thought is unidirectional and imbues materials with meanings but recognizes that – as a result of their ability to relate – materials enable, prompt and prohibit behaviour because of their essential and substantive materiality.

Malafouris (2013) adopts the notion of the extended mind to explain how materials affect people's thinking. Using ideas similar to those of Clark and Chalmers (1998) and Sheldrake (2004), Malafouris (2013) questions placing the mind within the confines of the human body exclusively and suggests that it extends further than the boundaries of the flesh. This conception presents understandings and knowledge as emergent-with materials, and as a result of being embedded within, or integral to, the rest of the material world. This is not, of course, to reject any symbolic attributions outright but is to embrace the role that materials play in articulating, mobilizing and influencing outcomes (for which read 'the way in which it can be related to') (Drazin and Küchler 2015). Vokes (2013), writing specifically of Ugandan practice, reminds us of the depth or embodied significance of material relationships, when he states that bodies are (seen as) composites that can be formed only through the exchange of vital, worldly materials (2013: 223). Iovino and Oppermann also see life as being rooted in 'narratives of matter' (2014: 13) and they remind us that 'the creative entanglements of agencies [should not be thought of as] only ways of world mirroring but [are] coemerging ways of world making' (2014: 14).

The ingredients of identity and place are, on first inspection, mythical and ephemeral (or immaterial) in this example. However, the meaning of the *fingo* results from the manner by which the materiality of the ingredients is able to act when they are together, and, therefore, should not be conceived of as a symbolic placemarker of meanings. On the contrary, it is how water behaves – it dissolves items, it evaporates and distils, thereby increasing its potency, coupled with its ability to soak into the soil – that accounts for the way in which the potion functions and can be understood.

The co-constituency of identity and place is well established (Cresswell 2004; Massey 2005). Obtaining permission or gaining the authority to reside in an area typically draws together both concepts, with one being used to validate and support the other. Moreover, using place to authenticate or negate identity claims is a frequently recurring theme historically, politically and ethnographically; indeed, this lens on identity is particularly potent in current affairs today. For self-proclaimed, territorially ambiguous migrants, as the Giriama appear to be, attachment to land is awkward and equivocal, as their place in a fixed, continuous and persistent landscape cannot be found. Without clear, unambiguous claims to an earthy material home, it appears that the Giriama, use or engage with water as the physical connection and constant that joins them to the past, their authentic selves and also the land that they now inhabit. Thus, the wet (potion) blended *with* the dry (land) producing a new muddy materiality (cf. Appadurai and Breckenridge 2009 (Wet Theory)) that blended the transported materials with the landscape on which they now found themselves. Rather than depict them as acting in opposition to the dry (cf. Dundes 1981) or degrading the land's dryness or dissipating or losing their essence, the Giriama present this event as a process of blending or becoming through the watery potion's absorption into the geography. Consequently, the authentic identity of the Giriama, held in suspension, enabled a material unity between the Giriama bodies of yesterday and today with the current landscape. When the pot smashed and the liquid soaked into the earth, the Giriama bound their concentrated collective identity to that place and thereby, through the joining of materials (Purpura 2009), were provided with a claim to a particular piece of geography and history. Furthermore, water's behaviour is mirrored in the Giriama narrative about their heritage. Water is material in flux. It moves through landscapes, travels and forms its own pathways, has one name but many faces, appropriates the ground it settles on and hides, only to reappear later in a different location – just as the Giriama have done.

In this chapter, we have seen how watery behaviours in a dry region physically and culturally shape the people who live there. By focusing on Giriama origin myths, water has been shown to be responsible for the articulation of contemporary local conceptions of identity, place and kin. Through the adoption of an NM framework, the materiality of water – what it can do in raised temperatures and in scant amounts – has influenced the value and meanings attributed to it. Therefore this chapter has illustrated how cultural meanings emerge with, and are predicated on, the brute materiality and methods that substances perform together. In this case, what water can do has been instrumental in shaping collective notions of Giriama authenticity as well as the physicality of individual bodies.

6 LANJARON, SPAIN

In this chapter we move away from a region in which water regularly disappears and 'hides' from people to one in which it slows down and virtually stops moving. In the last chapter we saw how carrying water across large distances shapes the bodies and minds of the people engaging with it in rural Kenya. In this chapter, watery relationships are reliant on encouragement, gentle coaxing, persuasion and careful attention to how water behaves at different times of year if the ecological landscape is to benefit from a regular, productive supply.

The climate varies dramatically across Spain. Typically, the north is considered to be quite wet, while the south – and particularly the south-eastern Mediterranean coast (where we are going now) – routinely experiences dry and hot seasons. Indeed, some areas of this region are defined as semi-desert. For example, Almeria, just a few kilometres to the east of Lanjaron, receives less than 150 millimetres of rainfall annually. As with that described in the previous chapter, the area relies on local earth systems for a supply of water – that is, water is not piped in from other locations, but must fall in the area to be used. Far from falling regularly, rainfall along the Spanish Mediterranean tends to be concentrated over brief periods, sometimes of just a few hours per year. Seasonal rains that fall and stay as snow on the higher ground, therefore, serve the region. Consequently, the water supply here is considered to be temporal or seasonal, because many months can pass with only negligible amounts of rainfall.

On first inspection, the example that we are going to study appears to be one of successful water management. However, the New Materialities (NM) perspective demonstrates how this example is not simply concerned with managing water but is illustrative of a form of ecological relationship that recognizes water's material behaviours as being co-constructively integral to the ecology of the location. In other words, this presents as a sensitively tuned partnership between people and water, which works simultaneously to support both humans' and water's requirements, rather than simply to provide water for people. This example also demonstrates how water's material behaviours are liable to shift and create alterations that demand that people invent novel behaviours to perpetuate sustainable relationships with it. Therefore, after looking at how water has shaped the way in which it can be engaged with, and how relationships with water in Lanjaron have moulded the landscape, we will see how water's seasonal activities have been instrumental in establishing the water culture for which Lanjaron is now becoming known.

Lanjaron is a small rural town, inland – less than 50 kilometres – from the Mediterranean 'Costa del Sol' coast. Situated 659 metres above sea level and with a population of approximately 3,500 people, the town looks out across the Mediterranean, towards the Atlas mountains of Morocco in North Africa. Positioned on the south-facing slopes of a mountainous area within the Sierra Nevada of Andalusia called Las Alpujarras, the town is similarly settled below snow-capped peaks as the African peaks which it looks at. The name 'Alpujarra' translates as 'mountains of whiteness' (Wright and Campbell 2008: 26) – a name that signposts the significance that is attributed to the snow in the area. It also references the significant Arab influences in the region. The name of the town – Lanjaron – reflects something of the location's material character. It is derived from the medieval Spanish or Castillio word *lanchar* (a word that is rarely used today), meaning 'to become overcast' and/or 'to freeze' (Castillio is similar to colloquial Latin). The Spanish tourist board, perhaps tenuously, claims that it is a reference to the location's abundant water supply (GranadaSpain.org 2017). Lanjaron's elevation and position on the south-west side of the range, south of the city of Granada, means that its weather is significantly different from that in the villages on the coast, and therefore it has more rain than areas lower down. The road to Lanjaron acts as something of a doorway into the string of villages that run along the southern flanks of the snowy mountains, culminating at one of the highest inhabited villages in Europe (Trevelez, at 1486 metres). Some of the twenty-three gentle summits that are visible on the approach to Lanjaron from Granada may be covered with snow until August or September each year. In the past, these peaks experienced perpetual snow, but changes in the climate since the 1990s have seen the snow cover fade at certain times of the year.

Due to the sharp rise or gradient of the land, Las Alpujarras is structured in such a way as to have a series of different altitudinal zones that produce climate pockets that run, almost like ribbons of crops, along the mountains. This supports an extensive variety of flora and fauna thriving in close proximity, which offers virtually unrestricted crop diversity and multiple growing seasons on each farm. Consequently, an alpine eco-system is available towards the tops of the ridges and there is an almost tropical climate down towards the sea. This means that, higher up the mountains, it is possible to grow chestnuts, pines and cherries, while lower down – sometimes in the same village – it is possible to harvest olives and citrus fruits. This is certainly the case for people living and farming in the region. A Lanjaron farmer might grow oranges and lemons on lower fields, olives and almonds a few terraces higher and then cherries and chestnuts on the highest ground.

Obviously, the fecundity of any area is not reliant on air temperature and sunlight alone: water is necessary too. With low annual rainfall at all levels on the slopes of Las Alpujarras, farmers must access enough water regularly for their crops to survive. Any rain falling on steep slopes tends to move quickly down to the river bed in the valley, leaving the soil on the slopes dry. Without the ability to draw rain to their fields as the Giriama discussed in Chapter 5 do through complicated rituals, the locals here instead work to coax or persuade water to flow over the fields at ordered intervals so as to enable it to cover a wider surface area and soak the earth. Thus it is not enough simply to bring the water from the upper elevations to the towns. A more nuanced approach is necessary in order to avoid the water travelling out and down to the sea too rapidly.

Encouraging water to adopt a path other than the one that it has chosen is a complex business that demands recognition of what the water needs in a given landscape, even with today's technological advances. As we have seen, water is a maverick substance that has the urge to move relentlessly, and uses multiple methods to achieve its compulsion to travel. In the eighth century, when the water system in Lanjaron was implemented, the locals must have paid very close attention to how water behaves both generally and within this geography, specifically to construct a system that still works and continues to be used across the region today. By acting in relationship with the flows and stores of water that are particular to this area (and the manner in which water inevitably inclines towards the sea), the Moorish and Berber populations of the past were able to produce what Wright and Campbell have called a 'hydraulic landscape' (2008: 26) – that is, one moved by water.

Slow water: glaciers, ice and snow

Because of the low temperatures at the top of the mountains, the water that falls there solidifies even before it reaches the ground and, consequently, in contrast to water falling in other locations with steep slopes, it is slow to move on from where it lands. The ice that sits cold and hard in the north-facing pockets of the mountains, and that is said to feed the many tarns (or lakes) near the peaks, is claimed to have been formed out of the glaciers left over from the so-called Little Ice Age (LIA) (Gómez-Ortiz et al. 2009). The dramatic decrease in temperatures across Europe in the 1300s is attributed to the LIA (Fagan 2001). Indeed, that this ice is here at all is used to substantiate the existence of the contentious LIA (Gómez-Ortiz et al. 2009). Locally, the lakes are called *Ojos del mar* (trans: 'eyes of the sea') because they were once thought to reflect the behaviour of the sea below.

The icy water around and in the lakes slowly filters down through the ground into the maze of underground fissures, splits, channels and aquifers that allow it to run through the body of the earth of the Sierra, where it eventually finds its way into the rivers in the valleys below. From there, it finally flows out into the Mediterranean Sea. Water moves incrementally faster as it warms up, which means that it is detained at the peaks before it slowly soaks into and spreads through the soil on its way down. Because it has not changed for hundreds of years, the glacial water that remains as ice is called 'dead ice' (Gómez-Ortiz et al. 2009), and its presence acts as both a store and a restraint that slows down water's movement from the top peaks to the sea. One might imagine that, with the sun beating down on the mountains day after day, the ice would melt quickly, but this is not the case. In any event, it is not the sun that melts ice; rather, it is the air temperature caused by the heat of the sun that does so. Thus, at higher altitudes, the melting point of ice in warmer air alters but, perhaps more importantly, it is the purity, transparency and the depth of glacial ice that stop it from melting away with any rapidity. Therefore, just like snow's whiteness bounces the sun back off it, ice has the ability to reflect light back again, thereby preventing it from melting (Cuffey and Patterson 2010 (see the *albedo* effect)). This means that it takes much longer for air temperatures to rise, which in turn means that it takes longer to melt the ice.

Reference to the permanent snow and ice that resembled stone in this area can be found in Arabic documents that go as far back as the twelfth century (Gómez-Ortiz et al. 2009: 283). The ice is described as having a special kind of allure, attributed to the similarities in consistency that it has to 'the hardest marble' (Madoz 1849, cited in Gómez-Ortiz et al. 2009: 285). Lying resistant, solid, sparkling and unyielding with and across the rocks, the enormous glacial fields of the Sierra are said to have shone eerily blue in places (Migues 2006). Glacial ice shines blue because of its age. It is not just compacted snow; it is denser and therefore creates a different crystalline structure from ice that is manufactured in a freezer. Glacial ice is also full of debris on account of the minerals accumulated as it scours the earth and rocks.

Contrary to expectations, however, rather than creating a worrying, alien landscape and impenetrable fortress that one might be at pains to avoid, the ice seems to have attracted people to the heights by means of its exceptional and intriguing materiality (cf. Bennett 2010). Consequently, snow and ice became a delightful novelty on the lower, hotter and drier slopes of the Sierra. The phenomenological brilliance of ice in the heat needs little explanation. We can simply imagine the sensorial pleasure that this cool material brought to people who had limited access to such cold, and that such novelty would be so desirable that it would eventually became economically significant (Brenan 2008) – and it did. Thus, numerous economic ventures associated with ice developed, along with a route into the peaks that is now called the *Camino de los Neveros* (Road of the Snow Harvesters). In due course, being a *Neveros* was an established profession. *Neveros* transported huge chunks of ice in baskets, using trains of mules to bring the weighty cargo off the slopes and into the towns. They worked during the night to avoid losses, and stored the ice in deep, stone-lined wells in the shade, insulated with straw. Other than as a cooling aid, ice was eventually traded to the ice cream makers who served the rich in Granada (Martínez 2014). Travelling into the ice was dangerous. Not only was the distance onerous and prohibitive, but the paths to the summits were notorious for freak accidents and violent attacks from the bandits who lived near the top of the peaks, hiding out beyond the reach of the law (Brenan 2008: 174). Nevertheless, it soon became lucrative.

Ice is one of the coldest naturally occurring edible materials, and was certainly uncommon for the populations who previously inhabited the lower slopes. The first recorded information about edible iced milky products arises from China during the Tang period (AD 618–907) (Weir 2015) and only later spread to Europe, including Spain (via Italy) through the Moorish population in the 1500s. In the sixteenth century, Italian ice cream was made by cooling cream and sugar over ice and salt (Smith 2007). However, prior to using milk, ice and fruit were mixed to create something akin to a refreshing sorbet. Today, what were once the ice pits of Lanjaron and Granada have been transformed into flamboyant *heladaría* (ice cream parlours), with a multitude of ice cream flavours to choose from.

Adding rock salt to ice 'intensifies the natural coldness of the ice' (Smith 2007: 314) and allows it to be used to freeze ingredients together fairly rapidly. For ice to be able to melt, it needs energy in the form of heat from the surrounding air to break the hydrogen bonds that are holding the water molecules together as a solid (ice). By adding salt to the ice, the melting point is altered. This is because the ice needs to find more heat to be able to melt, which, in turn, means that it melts more slowly. Its ability to retain its state is, of course, connected to its ability to preserve, which was significant, but is countered by its tendency to melt, move on and disappear. As we have seen already, water's quest for movement underpins every state that it adopts, which meant that water forced the snow harvesters to revisit the icy planes regularly.

As we can see, then, the relationship between the material molecularity of this slow water (that is, how water, as ice and snow, behaves in the cold) and the topography (that is, the steep slopes of Las Alpujarras) are accountable for one aspect of the shape of the area and the relationship between water and people. In addition to the quest to harness the properties and effects of cold, solid water, encouraging liquid waters both to flow across the land and to stay longer with people occupied much of the population's time. This is where we will turn our attentions to now.

In a region in which the climate can bring months of searing heat, the section of the Sierra Nevada and Las Alpujarras in which Lanjaron nestles presents as a patch of virtually unparalleled fertility and a picture of fresh abundance in an otherwise hot, dry and dusty area. In 1752, Murillo marvelled at it, indirectly referencing the continuous glacial ice and snows, when he stated that 'nature herself made an everlasting well' (cited in Gómez-Ortiz et al. 2009: 283) in Lanjaron. Around the same time, Ponz (1797) went so far as to draw a biblical connection to the landscape from its watery materiality:

> A gully filled with snow, considerably the first snow that fell after the Flood, turned to stone; as it lies open to the North, here there is ice where in other places there is only snow; and it never melts. (cited in Gómez-Ortiz et al. 2009: 285)

However, the fertility and greenness of the land cannot be attributable to just one aspect: it is not water alone but its relationships with the other materials, including the people of the area, that together form the ecology that has produced the abundance. Through working together with the land and the different kinds of waters of the mountain, the people who found themselves relocating to this terrain after the Christians managed to release their stronghold on Granada (Headworth 2004), are *together* responsible for encouraging diversity in the region. Thus, let us remind ourselves that it is the outcome of the relationships between all agents that co-generatively produces, and continues to shape, all regions – as it has with this one. Because it is necessary for people to physically interact with water on a regular basis, the daily activities of the people are bound to associate and cooperate with the way in which the water flows.

The Moorish influence: hydrologers

According to Amelang (2013), the Moorish or Berber influence on the Iberian Peninsula goes back as far as the year 711, when invaders overcame the Visigoths who inhabited the land mass that was not yet established as Spain (Hispania). In 1492, after hundreds of opulent and economically stable years of coexistence, the Christian Inquisition expelled the *Morisco* (the collective name for Moors and

Berbers) and the resident Jewish population (Amelang 2013). Their collective rejection from the area was part of a process known as the *Reconquista* – a ruthless, indomitable and often violent process that was rooted in a rejection of religious differences that had occurred over hundreds of years across Europe. Prior to 1492, most people living in Iberia were Muslims and the situation was one of 'mutual toleration' rather than hostility (Amelang 2013: 14–15). Nevertheless, after years of intractable fighting across the peninsula, most of the Islamic influence was pushed from the north southwards. When Granada finally fell, the total ejection of the *Morisco* from Iberia was stifled when the southern slopes of the Sierra Nevada (in other words, Las Alpujarras, including the village of Lanjaron) was given as a 'peace offering' (and compensatory fiefdom on account of its lack of value), to 'Boadil (the last Moorish ruler of Granada)' (Wright and Campbell 2008: 25). This singular deed of banishment allowed thousands of evicted Muslims to shelter in the then somewhat inhospitable mountains, where they went on to construct what amounted to replicas of Moroccan farming villages on the very steep and dry slopes. Already recognized as expert hydrologists – as evidenced in the watery paradisiacal palaces that they had previously established in Granada and other locations – they began negotiating with the local water sources so as to coax water into their lives. Their methods, directly linked to their knowledge and understanding of how water behaves in arid regions, meant that they went on to develop a spectacularly simple and effective web of water channels and pathways that still function across the region today (de Châtel 2015; Wilson 2004). As we will now see, it was both their presence in Las Alpujarras and the manner by which water behaved in this region that established the delicate and sensitive irrigation system that still feeds most of the area today (Wilson 2004).

The Moors and the Berbers are often depicted as having an unparalleled understanding of water behaviours and an unmatched ingenuity with regard to hydro-technology (de Châtel 2015). As was shown in Chapter 5, the Giriama women whose lives are occupied with water haulage hold low status. In contrast, de Châtel, citing Aly Mazaheri (2015: 46), demonstrates that, in other dry lands, water, hydrographers, hydrocultures and methods of relating to water are valued highly above other items and knowledge. Typically, in wetter climates it is land ownership that is synonymous with wealth, whereas, as de Châtel (2015) shows, in arid regions, being able to influence water creates power and capital. Perhaps as a result, the Persian Arabic word 'irrigation' (*apady*) evolved to mean 'village' (de Châtel 2015).

Of note is that there is some disagreement about how the system in Lanjaron and surrounding areas emerged. Wilson (2004) maintains that there is some uncertainty concerning who is responsible for the water system, querying whether it is of Roman or Arabic origin. Citing Wittfogel's hypothesis of Oriental despotism and hydraulic societies (1957) that maintains that substantial irrigation systems such as this one demand centralized control, Wilson (2004) remains unsure. Consequently, he suggests that such systems may have been constructed piecemeal through simple local co-operation rather than as a result of any despotic ruling. On the other hand, de Châtel (2015) is certain, and directly links Arab water relationships in other countries with these methods in Spain.

Invisible waters

Only a very small percentage of global water runs over the ground or fills the rivers or lakes that human settlements congregate around to use. Most of the water that falls as rain on the earth soaks down through the soil and away from the surface, to become ground water. Rain falling as drops puddles and penetrates into the earth, where, through a process of percolation, the underground stores of water become recharged. On its travels, the water is filtered through the different types of rock, sand and soil in the area, thus altering its mineral content. Once past root level and protected by clay soil or rock, it remains secreted, held and sheltered under the ground, sometimes simply in the soil, and sometimes in vast, rocky aquifers, hidden from view and immediate access. Some of the water held in aquifers has been there for millions of years, however, increasingly, there are concerns that it has barely sat for fifty years and is being depleted on account of the rate at which it is being drawn out of the ground (Gleeson et al. 2015). If groundwater is depleted and not enabled to recharge, it runs out – as we are seeing across the world today (e.g. California and Las Vegas). On steep slopes, ground water can emerge as spring water at different points in the landscape as a result of channels forming outlets. In the case of Lanjaron water, the slow glacial melts (headwater) feed the springs that emerge above and around the town.

To bring hidden or invisible water up to the surface, one must first locate the underground aquifer. This is done by simply drilling down into the ground after studying the surrounding soil and flora for indications of water being present. In the past this was achieved by placing a piece of wax-coated wool into a hole in the ground during the night. 'Placing the wool in a hole in the ground overnight, they would cover it with a small bowl. If the wool was damp in the morning, it was a sign of water's presence' (de Châtel 2015: 43). 'As Mazaheri explained, the biblical phrase "seek and you will find" stems from the Persian original "Dig and you will reach the water"' (de Châtel 2015: 43).

Using these ancient methods, in the 1500s, the local Arab population devised a method to bring the water from the snows above and the underground aquifers into a delicate system or network of metre-wide water channels called *acequias*. The system is designed to encourage the water to spread its influence by taking multiple detours on its route to the sea. Thus, instead of moving directly into the valley once it emerges from under the ground, the snow melt is encouraged to take a much longer circuitous route along the edges of the many terraces that were constructed to create flat land out of the steep slopes. It is these diversions that are responsible for making the dry soil of the mountains in this area as wet and fertile as they are (Headworth 2004).

> Several of these villages owe their existence to a system of watering extending back a thousand years, where snowmelt from the high sierra to the north of these villages is conducted along high level carriers (acequias) to locations above the villages. Some of this water supplies fountains which can be distinctive features of the villages. Most of it soaks into the ground, being spread over gentle slopes or discharged into recharge ponds dug into the hillsides. Water in the acequias can also be released via control structures into smallholdings below.
> (Headworth 2004: 166)

The system, ecological in design, does not use any pipes or pumps to move the melt and aquifer water down into the fields and villages. More importantly it recognizes water's materiality and its complex material behaviours and, significantly, does not focus on getting water to people for human use exclusively but rather recognizes the need for water to soak across and into the land in order for the venture to be successful.

Using only gravity and the cambers and contours along the courseways to ensure a gradient current, the original earthy channels were dug in such a way as to allow the water to spread transversely and be retained in the landscape, rather than (as one might assume) be directed pointedly to certain locations for storage. To support this project, families lined the sides of their terraces with stone, creating walls that cooled the soil, encouraged the water to pool and discouraged evapo-transpiration, thereby allowing the water to soak down into, rather than run off, the soil. The retained water was then able to filter back down into the ground water and aquifers. In recognition that water must spread its influence, this method sustained the landscape and supported the water to be shared more equitably. The aim, therefore, was not objectively focused on getting enough water to each farm but was designed to increase the coverage, reach and diffusion of the water across the slopes. Consequently, instead of commandeering the water for human use exclusively, the design supported the other existing springs (*fuentes*) across the region being replenished during long periods without rain. These ancient stone walls still actively maintain the water content of each terrace and are visible as vast striations of stone running along the landscape from right across the valley.

As already noted, the value of dry land over water is positioned by de Châtel (2015) as a fundamental difference between conceptions of the material world. She even goes so far as to claim that the value of water is higher than land in drier regions. Her assessment could account for the decision of the incoming Christians to hand Las Alpujarras over to the outgoing Muslims after the Reconquest; as it was a desiccated area, the Christians may well have perceived it as being less valuable initially. Regardless, it took only another seventy-six years before its value was recognized and the villagers were forcibly evicted. According to Wright and Campbell (2008), over 12,000 Christian families were moved in to take advantage of the now-established fecundity and to remove what was considered to be the barrier of Islamic influence that was perceived to run uncomfortably through the mountains just south of Granada. Perhaps in reference to the conflict between faiths that took place over these waters, the river Guadalfeo that runs from the snowy heights to the coast means 'river of faith' in Arabic (Wright and Campbell 2008: 26). We will come back to this point later when we revisit the annual water fight that is celebrated in Lanjaron each year. First, let us turn our attention to the dynamic capacity of the water itself.

Not all waters are equal

The water that emerges from the rocks in Lanjaron has journeyed from the high glacial peaks of Mulhacén and Veleta to the town. Other than the peaks of the Alps, Mulhacén is the highest mountain in western Europe and is named after Abu l-Hasan Ali, one of the last Muslim kings of Spain. Filtering through the earth and collecting minerals as it travels, the water emerges from each spring 'full' and with its own character on account of the long journey that it has taken. Even to this day, its route avoids any contact with human activities because, in 1986, the United Nations Educational, Scientific and Cultural Organization (UNESCO) declared the Sierra a biosphere reserve, thereby banning any industrial activity in the area and essentially preserving it (UNESCO-MAB 2007). Furthermore, as there is no river feed to the springs, it is the water that fell as snow and soaked into the ground many years ago (and has not seen the light of day) that surfaces around the town.

Lanjaron has over sixty-seven documented places where water springs from the ground without human intervention. Most of these water sources flow with cold water and are established as public fountains (*fuentes*), which are available free of charge for the people in the town. However, a few of the outlets produce less appealing sulphurous, almost thick, yellow-brown water that forms into thermal pools, surrounded by stalactites of hardened depositions dripping from the mouth of the spring. The water from the source named '*Salud*' (health) has been bottled and sold since the late 1800s, after the water was recognized for its mineral content and purported health-generating qualities. This – coupled with the town's hot springs and other outlets where the water emerges with different mineral quantities – means that the town's name is now synonymous with water in Spain. Consequently, Lanjaron bottled mineral water is not only acknowledged as being healthy; it is also considered curative, and therefore numerous people come to the town specifically to collect it. However, now, unfortunately, only three of the *fuentes* continue to yield untreated mineral water. Disappointingly, the rest run water that is processed and chlorinated by the local sanitation unit. Nevertheless, people are known to travel miles to be cured by the Lanjaron waters in the *Baniero* (spa). The word 'spa' is a Latin acronym for *solus per aquam* ('only through water') or *salus per aquam* ('health through water').

While Samos claims that the 'medicinal use [of Lanjaron's waters] . . . could go back to the Middle Ages', he also acknowledges that 'there is . . . no written record of the curative use of water beyond the last third of the eighteenth century' (2006: 148), if we are to go by the words of Dr Medina Estévez (1864):

> Certainly, in the year 1774, coincidence in the form of divine inspiration, remembering the time of the Greeks, made a dying man drink the water of one of the many springs that soften this population. In imitation of him, others followed his example with the same and different diseases, and achieved a healthy effect, forming with his testimony a clear and unequivocal proof . . . Ailments, resisted before the other hygienic and therapeutic aids. And, behold, waters which had hitherto been regarded as noxious, had become an obvious remedy.
>
> (cited in Samos 2006: 148)

In conversation, locals substantiate and even augment Estévez's story claiming that the special properties of the water were accidentally realized by a sickly medieval monk travelling in Las Alpujarras. According to these stories, the monk, close to death, and in terrible pain and suffering from some undocumented condition, noticed that small birds died after they drank from the spring that emerges, brown and smelly, near the Moorish castle just below the town. Hoping for swift release, he, too, drank the water, only to find that it had the opposite effect on him. He survived and, indeed, was cured of his ailment. The locals had avoided this water due to its appearance and odour. This event helped the town to realize that the water was medicinal.

Mineral water: healing and destruction

> The water therefore 'has definitively marked the place, enhancing its agrarian wealth and creating new expectations.
> (Samos 2006: 149)

Martínez-Reguera (1896, cited in Eyzaguirre 2006) documents the long history associated with achieving recognition of the potential of this water. Unlike Lourdes, where any miraculous effect of the water is based in a Christian story, this water story is Arabic in origin and has received less appreciation and publicity. It took from the 1700s until the beginning of the twentieth century for a series of dedicated individuals to push for its status. Even with regular analysis that persuasively determined its mineral content, the notion of gaining benefit from drinking smelly water or lying in the hot, discoloured spring waters was underappreciated, despite the water emerging at a comfortable 23°C from the rocks. Bathing and even bathrooms were associated with paganism and, as a result, baths and bathrooms were not features in medieval Christian homes (despite any Roman influences) (Girón Irueste 2006). Bathrooms were thought to be items that one might find in Muslim or Jewish homes and were therefore avoided as places of evil or scandalous deeds that one could associate with pagan body worshiping. Only sick people could take to the water if advised (Girón Irueste 2006) and, consequently, few Christians in Lanjaron would have considered any water for bathing, let alone the hot, discoloured spring water on their doorsteps. Thus, rather than for general health-maintaining properties, the water was initially promoted as a curative or medicinal substance for the sick. However, increased attention to hydrology across Europe in the 1800s and the subsequent scientific analysis of the waters as a result (Migues 2006), later kindled recognition of the potential (economic and otherwise) of the water, which in turn resulted in local authorities attempting to 'clean up', or even sanitize, the water to make it more desirable for the consumer (Eyzaguirre 2006; Samos 2006). It was this that began a new relationship between Lanjaron people and the surrounding water – one whereby control of the water was established through claims of expertise (medical and otherwise), as the following text, signed by royalty in 1816, demonstrates:

Among the many and precious gifts with which providence favoured Spain, one should consider the abundance of mineral waters distributed at various points along its vast expanse . . . [there should be] a person who, with knowledge of its effects on the various ailments, knows how to retain some and direct others in the use . . . The lack of such persons is very common in the mineral waters of the peninsula, and this consideration and that of their fatal results afflict my heart. In order to remedy such a grave evil, and as long as circumstances allow me to carry out the plans I am contemplating in order to improve this important branch in a whole, I have come to resolve that in each of the most reputable baths of the kingdom be established a teacher of sufficient knowledge of the virtues of its waters, and of the medical part necessary to know how to determine its application and use. These places will be of fixed and indispensable residence; Shall enjoy an allowance of five thousand reales annually, paid from the funds of their own and from the immediate people to the baths . . . with the obligation to assist the poor who attend, and freedom to demand . . . of the affluent patients. They . . . shall pay particular attention to the aptitude and ability of the aspirants to acquire the chemical knowledge of the waters, and of the rest with respect to their application . . . Signed of the Royal Hand of S. M. In the Palace on June 29, 1816.
(Eyzaguirre 2006: 128)

This was a dramatic departure from working with the water, as the Moors had done, to a practice in which the people attempted to shape, contain and direct it for exclusively human purposes. Scientific analysis of each spring resulted in a catalogue of different benefits for the human body, through both ingestion and application. For example, the water of the Capuchin can be used as a 'laxative, purgative and tonic . . . [for] dyspepsia, anorexia, gastrodynia [when made up into decoctions with] . . . honey, apiary, cider bark syrup . . . [and] cinnamon' (Eyzaguirre 2006: 129) to aid digestion. While the waters of Capilla, are useful as a 'tonic, astringent and diuretic' (Eyzaguirre 2006: 129) on account of its iron content, Salud 'is useful to refresh the blood and to temper . . . heat and fiery temperaments' (Eyzaguirre 2006: 129).

According to the Spanish tourist board, the people of Lanjaron have been recognized by the World Health Organization (WHO) as having the highest life expectancy in the world (Lanjaron n.d.), which the locals attribute to their health-inducing water and the wide variety of crops that their location enables. Furthermore, this and the Mayor's novel move in 1999, which made it officially illegal to die in Lanjaron (a bid to draw Granada council's attention to the town's restrictions concerning cemetery space), ties or tangles the water and the bodies of the population together in a unique picture of health, longevity and materiality – something that had been recognized in the early 1800s.

> Placed the town in such an advantageous position that it frees you from the frozen air of the North and from the humidity, and from excessive heat and cold . . . Supplied with a pure, clear and crystalline water, endowed with a living, fresh and pleasant taste . . . Favored in such happy circumstances, it is easy to foresee that they should enjoy complete health, as they really enjoy. Do not know endemic and epidemic diseases, but sporadic or common to all the inhabitants of the globe. The intermittent fever, so common in humid and swampy places, does not suffer here: the chronic gastric conditions typical of countries where drinking water is bad, are not observed in this . . . They grow strong, healthy and vigorous. Digest quickly and easily.
> (Baldovi 1824 (employed as Director of the Spa in 1818), cited in Eyzaguirre 2006: 132)

But the water is not *only* responsible for bringing life-enhancing features to the town; locals are also aware of its destructive abilities. The reason that Lanjaron has water one can call 'mineral' and 'health inducing' is the rock formations through which the water filters. Being situated at the junction of two types of rock offers Lanjaron one topographical explanation for these ancient waters being able to pour out as readily and as rich in minerals as they do. However, unfortunately, the structure of the landscape in the region is also prone to seismic movements, some of which have been known to destroy buildings all the way to Malaga (Samos 2006). This, in addition, to the flash flooding and high winds that can lash destructively at the area, causing two deaths as recently as December 2016 (Davies 2016), means that the people of Lanjaron are also aware of the damaging capabilities of the local waters.

Documentation dating from 1995 shows that many of the perpetual snows at which early writers marvelled have gone and the enormous fields of ice that once shone on the tops of the peaks have vanished. Consequently, these material changes result in the water moving faster through and away from the area. This, and the deforestation of the higher slopes, is said to contribute to amplified sedimentation rates and increased run-off (Durán Zuazo et al. 2012), which is also causing the quality of the water (that is, its contents) to change (Durán Zuazo et al. 2012). In addition, modern alterations to the ancient water system – specifically the practice of cementing parts of the channels to prohibit water loss – is preventing the water from behaving as it once did (Edgeworth 2011; Herrera Wassilowsky 2011). According to Headworth (2004), this is both problematic and a mistake because it reduces the ability of the water to filter through and recharge the ground water on which the lower levels rely.

Change: festivities and water

Every Spanish town periodically celebrates a significant occasion with a fiesta. Fiestas are synonymous with Spain and consequently draw huge numbers of tourists into the country each year to experience the spectacles that take place on fiesta nights. Across Andalusia, on the night of 23 June, the fiesta *La Noche de San Juan* celebrates the beginning of the heat of the summer – and it is no different in Lanjaron. Across the Christian world, the Night of Saint John is celebrated using fire. As the day fades into night, bonfires are lit for people to jump over and purify themselves. In Lanjaron, however, they use water instead of fire. One could claim that this is actually more appropriate, as it is consistent with John the Baptist's purported practice of baptism by total immersion in water. However, in this case, it is the materiality of water and how it behaves in this geography at this time of year that accounts for the use of water in the fiesta.

The ritual

The day before the night of 23 June, the whole town prepares for the fiesta. The church doors are barred and covered with protective plastic sheets. The people who own the buildings that line the main road through the town work hard to protect their properties because they know that, on the stroke of midnight – as the shortest night of the year begins – the streets will fill with water and the town will be inundated, washed and saved from the potential destruction of a real flood.

As the clock moves towards midnight, the streets begin to fill with people all working towards the western side of the town. The aim of the night is to get from one end of the town to the other by negotiating the many violent jets of water that are regularly positioned along the path designed to impede people's progress. Thousands of people from all over Spain accumulate at the starting point – some dressed up in elaborate and humorous fancy-dress costumes, but most in minimal clothing in anticipation of what is to come. For most participants the aim is simply to survive and get to the finish line, but some individuals take the occasion very seriously and hope to overcome the water and arrive first.

At the outset, everyone is comfortably dry, but they know that this will not last long. The drama to come causes obvious consternation as the crowd waits for the stroke of the clock that signals when the night moves into the beginning of a new day. Everyone gets into position so as to be ready to dowse others as soon as the signal is given at midnight. The waiting makes people twitchy, and as each participant has some kind of weapon – a bucket, pistol or plastic bottle – they make ready to drench and shock the person next to them with a view to obstructing their progress towards the other end of the town. During the dry period running up to the start of the ritual, the tension mounts palpably. Onlookers, safe above the now very fidgety and keen participants, on their balconies looking over the street, tease the crowd by jetting small streams of water from hoses and water pistols on to them. The crowd roars as the small drops of water hit, both in outrage at an early wetting and also in anticipation of the deluge to come. Everyone knows that water is going to penetrate into everything and flow everywhere, that there will be a struggle to negotiate it and that it will be impossible to escape it. The chance of any part of a participant's body avoiding total saturation is extremely unlikely. Indeed, everything in the water's path will be inundated, immersed and utterly unable to avoid contact with the water almost immediately. Everyone accepts that the water will be in control – not just making contact, but also pushing everyone unrelentingly, without discrimination or method to appeal. The water, gushing from the town's hydrants in vast hoses, will also spread its influence through the actions of all the contributors. Consequently, in its literature the *Ayuntamento* (the local council) advises participants to bring nothing of value to the ritual.

When a council official sounds the horn and the town erupts into action, the locals operating the hydrants near to the start line immediately blast the crowd with intense, joltingly violent, jets of water that force people to stagger from the strength of the discharge. Any notion of being able to keep dry is immediately washed from people's minds. Soaked to the skin, with cold water dripping from them, means that the journey has started. Everyone turns on each other, recognizing that they must survive and that they are in competition with each other. Consequently, and with blatant disregard for normal behaviour, whatever water is available is unremorsefully projected towards the nearest person. Each body seems to jar with the shock of being targeted, but in recognition of the intention to obstruct the other's passage retaliates by throwing more water. Now, drenched, disorientated, slipping and sliding with wet hair stuck to their faces, people realize that they must keep moving with the crowd. Screaming and yelling, with bodies sodden, flapping wet fabric and hair against each other, jostling, pushing and bumping together, the body of the crowd slides explosively and dangerously but excitedly, with each individual scrabbling in an attempt to supersede the next. Together, the bodies seem almost to meld – as though, in the saturated rush, they merge to resemble a wild, turbulent stream of splashing, dancing fluid water people hastening along a channel to a destination.

The distance from one end of the town to the other is not far to walk on an ordinary day, but, for a 'stream' of people, the journey becomes elongated, lubricated and liquid. In association, the expanse or space that comprises the town changes to one in which people pour down every street, exploding with exuberance like water flowing in an *acequia*. Local literature describes the event as a 'fight'. However, from doing the run, I would say that this description does little to describe the phenomenology of experiencing the event. This is not combat between people and water; rather, it is a process that mimics just how the constructed water system – and the liquid itself – materially enacts and *produces* the town with the people and the things that it passes through. Most importantly, the ritual illustrates the fragile yet indivisible relationship that articulates between water and people; how, together, they generate the forms of their lives; and how damage could be wrought if relationships disregard the inherent material forces that are obvious in both human and watery bodies.

All rituals employ deep and rich symbolism to effect (Bowie 2006). The methods and symbols used in rituals are claimed to be multi-vocal tools designed to increase the reach of the meaning to as many people as possible without a call to direct explanation (Van Gennep 2004). Therefore, ritual performances teach and perpetuate social behaviours and meanings through their symbolic ambiguity. This is achieved by leaving phenomenological interpretations to be arrived at individually (Van Gennep 2004). Consequently, the symbolism articulated in a ritual performance must be *felt* by the participants rather than being understood only intellectually. Furthermore, as ritual meanings are grasped physically or materially (at body level rather than just cognitively), they are more often than not notoriously challenging to express verbally. When this occurs, people claim to be able to understand but are unable to put their ideas into words without causing something of the feeling to degrade. This makes the feeling difficult to explain to others whilst also being simultaneously personally significant in a peculiar but potent way (Coxhead 1985). This can cause the experience to be more impactful and meaningful than ones that can be explained away easily.

In the case of the San Juan water event in Lanjaron, one almost becomes with (cf. Haraway 2008) the water during the ritual. This is because the method prompts participants to become like water in their passage to the finish line. Regularly positioned along the pathway are individuals whose purpose, it seems, is to constrain one's progress, but in fact they guide one onwards – just like the incoming flows of water in the *acequia* system that feed the town. Thus, the journey moves in rumbustious swells that are punctuated by determined and violent currents that might hold one back or direct one forward. One has to struggle hard to get past the obstacles, while remaining aware of the surrounding swell of bodies, and one knows that one must keep moving to avoid a problem. Triumphant when an obstacle is circumnavigated, one is then confronted with a new obstacle around the next corner. The whole town participates in the event – if not to throw water from their balconies at the river of people flowing below them, to offer the 'swimmers' some sustenance (local ham and hot chocolate) or other encouragement en route. Water swirls around the central streets of the town like a minor tsunami: even windows as high as the second storey of the tall town buildings are soaked. The water behaves in keeping with expectations and it penetrates everything in its path, thereby reminding people of its methods and manner.

A syncretic blend of pagan and Christian influences is evident in many Spanish fiestas. Pagan deities are often animated environmental elements such as fire, water or rocks (Dow 1996), and indirect worship of these elements is often tangentially (but potently) present in Spanish Christian fiestas. The famous tomato-throwing fiesta and the bulls of Pamplona are illustrative of this – as is the fiesta of *Patum* in Berga, recently recognized by UNESCO as an example of intangible heritage. The *Patum* lasts over a series of days and sees the *pueblo* come alive with action – inhabited by numerous giant puppets, fireballs, dancing and a relentless, haunting drum beat (hence the name of the festival is *pa-tum*, recreating the sound of the drum) that commences on the night of the Corpus Christi (Noyes 2003). Similarly, the Lanjaron fiesta mixes pagan with Christian ideas, thus establishing a link with pre-Christian ideals of the region and also acknowledging the community's inextricable material connection to water.

By the mid-sixteenth century, as a result of the pressure on *Moriscos* and the 'War of Granada' (Amelang 2013: 15), remaining populations were encouraged to 'relinquish their distinctive language, dress, festivities and other cultural practices' (Amelang 2013: 15). However, as each location fell under Christian rule in a piecemeal fashion, so, too, were the directives. Thus, according to Amelang (2013), any remaining *Moriscos* were given a chance to convert, and those who did were permitted to remain. However, rather than a blanket event, the directive was interpreted locally and creatively, which culminated in some established traditions melding with the incoming ideas rather than being entirely removed.

Lanjaron's water ritual is an example of the indomitable influence of the environmental factors of a location over the people, coupled with the cultural and historical changes through which the population have lived. This is almost visible as an imperceptible liquid thread running through their actions. Right at the point in the calendar at which water acquisition and retention become imperative, the people of this town have decided to demonstrate their ongoing relationship with the local water by allowing it to flow, without obstruction or control, out from the reserves held by the town. One might assume this to be a wasteful activity. Thoughtlessly allowing vital litres of water to flow down through the drains rather than over the fields seems foolish, at first sight. Equally, it could be judged an act of conspicuous consumption through which one advertises one's wealth in water to neighbouring villages. However, according to locals, it is neither of those things. Rather, it is an act of sensitivity and understanding that emerges from their material relationship with water, because water must be allowed to flow at the point in the year when the snows start to melt more quickly. At this point in the calendar, any reserves could likely be strained by the quickening extra melt, and thus the water itself demands releasing. According to locals, this is a relatively new ritual. As the influence of the spa decreased during the 1970s and 1980s, and the coastal towns such as Malaga and Marbella grew in popularity for tourists, Lanjaron looked for a way to draw people back to its streets. However, this also coincided with the perpetual snow decline as global air temperatures rose and climate change began to exert its influence (Durán Zuazo et al. 2012), causing the reserves of held water to strain at this time of year. Thus, in a perpetual dance with the liquid, Lanjaron's water ritual not only recognizes the materiality and behaviour of the water, but also responds to its needs and frees it from any constraints so that any damage to the system is avoided.

Rather than being in control of the water – as is often suggested in discussions about water systems (for example, see McCully 2001 and Strang 2014) – the behaviour of the population of Lanjaron (and the number of visitors that frequent the festival) is actively shaped by the materiality and physical behaviours of the water in this area. This is not simply a symbolic or causal relationship but one that is generated together and is the particular product of being in a physical relationship in which one partner's requirements affect the other (cf. Latour 2005). This example demonstrates how physicality and causality run contrary to expectations. In this case, material behaviours have altered in concert with a tangible sensitivity to impacting and surrounding conditions so as to produce cultural practices such as the ritual of *La Noche de San Juan*, the sharing and distribution of water and using different waters for healing purposes in Lanjaron.

7 WELSH WATER
The Resourcefulness of Water

Water is an 'uncooperative commodity' . . . There is something emotive – essential – in the nature of water, in the idea of water, which militates against it being owned and controlled for profit.
(Coopey and Tvedt 2006: iv)

Few things express dominance over other species as clearly as damming and redirecting flows of water to give primacy to human needs. Yet despite growing opposition, dams – especially large ones – are still presented triumphantly, as symbols of successful nationhood and economic development . . . they represent not only a competition for wealth, but also an aspiration for control over life itself and the vitality of 'living water.'
(Strang 2013b: 161)

In this chapter we consider the socio-material consequences of arresting flows and diverting river courses to create large, contained bodies of water. By examining the materiality of water when it is trapped, we will see how water *en masse* gains a potency or liquid force that builds as it accumulates. Therefore, we will explore the way in which water's power can amplify as it is trapped or collected in one area, and in doing so will recognize how water's material behaviours co-productively articulated and mobilized transformations in how the Welsh and the English relate to each other.

Water is paradoxically experienced as being simultaneously light, soft and weighty. It feels insubstantial as it nimbly slips through our fingers but when it is in a bucket – 'collectively' – it becomes bulky, substantial and heavy. This material paradox transpires simply because, in liquid form, it is ungraspable by human hand. Water simply flows off and away from objects that it does not soak into. This means that while one can get a sense of wetness from water, one can get a measurement of the weight of water only when it is detained within a container. Getting a sense of the force that water exerts can be experienced during the process of containing it: as more water fills a bucket, it becomes substantial and able to pull against us. This is in marked contrast to when one is swimming in a pool, for example. It is difficult to get a sense of the pressure that is being exerted by the water on our bodies when we are swimming in it. Despite the almighty weight of the water in a swimming pool, our bodies do not register its pressure as they would with a similarly weighted substance landing on us if we were on land. Water's pressure or force therefore amplifies when contained. Once contained, restricted and unable to easily move out of an area, the weight of water and the forceful material power that it is able to exert can be both quantified and produced.

This chapter explores how damming, restraining and controlling Welsh water by arresting and redirecting its flow played a part in shaping a revival or intensification of Welsh nationalist strength. Rather than presenting the ability to dam as a human activity that asserts dominance over planetary resources, the New Materialities (NM) perspective reminds us that the materiality of interacting substances plays an influential and formative role in shaping the manner that material engagements can articulate. As has been covered previously, it is because water does not fall equally on land and insists on moving that people must relentlessly attempt to contain and store it in a bid to create water security. Consequently, *it is the manner by which water behaves and people's dependence on it that governs* how relationships can form. Therefore, dams come into being because of what water does, as much as because of what people do. Correspondingly, not only does the perceived need to, and action of, damming water mould the shape of the lives of people; it also alters the course of the water, and thereby shapes a routine that would not have manifested itself without the circumstances of the relationship. Therefore, how water is, and how people are, presents as a performance possibility that can exist as it does only as a result of what the impacting materialities produce in that setting.

Establishing Welsh water: then and now

> It's a relief to hear the rain. It's the sound of billions of drops, all equal, all equally committed to falling, like a sudden outbreak of democracy. Water when it hits the ground instantly becomes a puddle or rivulet or flood.
>
> (Oswald 2012)

Wales has the reputation of being a wet country. According to the UK's Meteorological Office, the Welsh climate provides over 3,000 millimetres of rain annually (Metoffice.gov.uk 2017). Compared with rainfall in other parts of the British isles, this amount is actually not exceptional. For example, Scotland and parts of the north of England have similar levels. However, Welsh geographical features and the westerly location of the country both support its reputation as a country that is notably wet from rain.

Situated on the west coast of the British isles and surrounded on three sides by seas, Wales is described as having a temperate maritime climate, which is one that is affected by the oceans' airflow. All western coastal regions of higher latitudes are considered to have oceanic or maritime climates. Temperate maritime climates do not fluctuate between extreme seasonal changes. Thus, such climates are typically mild and cool for most of the year, without much variation, and, certainly, in the case of Wales, have a tendency to experience regular rain. The Welsh climate is topographically influenced by the significant amount of upland areas that it possesses (Macdonald et al. 2010). This is evident from the ancient spine of mountains that run up and down the length of the country. The spine includes three ranges: Snowdonia in the north; the Cambrian mountains that run from north to south, close to the coast; and the Brecon Beacons, situated towards the border with England in the east. The likelihood of precipitation is raised along with the height of the land above sea level. The chance of rain is higher in Wales on account of the coastal air being forced to rise from sea level into the hills rapidly and abruptly (Macdonald et al. 2010). Air rising cools quickly as it ascends, which encourages the moisture in the air to drop as rain. Consequently, the vegetation on the hills in Wales tends to remain a lush, energetic or dynamic green – or *gwyrdd* – most of the year round. (The traditional use of the word *gwyrdd* is problematic to translate directly in English, as it can be used to describe things that might equally be thought of as being green, blue or grey – particularly a pale blue or a greenish blue. *Glas* is the Welsh word for 'blue' but it, too, can be used to describe certain shades of what some would call 'green'. For example, the word for 'grass' translates as 'blue straw' (*glaswellt*). *Gwyrdd* is also understood as describing things that are 'lively and fresh'.)

The Welsh Government advertises the water in Wales as a feature of the country (Welsh Government 2017a). Its website boasts of 398 natural lakes (some miles long) alongside another ninety constructed across the small country (Welsh Government 2017a). (Wales is only 256 kilometres long and 96 kilometres wide, making an area of 20,777 square kilometres in total (Welsh Government 2017b).) Moreover, Welsh waterfalls, some higher than Niagara Falls, are offered as splendid natural spectacles for tourists to visit (Welsh Government 2017a). In addition to the portfolio of water opportunities for tourists, the locals also benefit from their water. The Welsh take pride in the fact that their water board is a not-for-profit organization whose slogan reads: 'Not for profit. For you' (*Dŵr Cymru* 2017). The company, named simply *Dŵr Cymru* (Welsh Water), is devoid of shareholders. Therefore all its profits return to the organization, both to improve the system and to ensure that bills remain comparatively low. In conversation with Geraint (2017), who works for *Dŵr Cymru*, I was told that workers and customers alike feel part of the company because the water is 'owned by us' (Geraint 2017 (pers. comm.)). This is an exceptional situation when compared with that in the rest of the UK, and one that comes as the result of a number of decisions made by the Welsh for *their* water, despite any directives to the contrary from England.

In a bid to move away from social dependency and what was labelled the 'nanny state' so as to create wealth through the profits of privately owned business, the Conservative Government of 1989 under Margaret Thatcher privatized water and (no pun intended) floated water authorities on the stock market that same year. Along with all the other British regional water authorities, Welsh Water was privatized in the same year. In 2000, after a decade of financial success, the company (now named Hyder) sold off its assets after experiencing financial trouble. From this, Welsh Water was sold to a public benefit company called *Glas Cymru* for £1. A year later, Welsh Water separated itself from other British privately owned water companies by declaring itself to be not for profit – an action that returned it to a state similar to its previous pre-privatization status. That Welsh Water is not privatized today is politically significant, as we will see later.

Nevertheless, one is still able to buy Welsh water. In keeping with the global demand for mineral water, and just as numerous other countries have done, Wales has taken advantage of consumer demand by bottling the water that materializes from springs of the Cambrian mountains. Claiming that its clarity and purity results from the filtration processes that occur as it travels through the ancient rocks of Wales, the Welsh have produced arguably one of the most famous, internationally recognized brands of water in recent years – *Tŷ Nant* water – which is most recognizable because of its distinctive bright blue glass bottle.

The language of water

> When people talk about the weather, one of the topics that is discussed most frequently is memory of past extreme weather events.
> (Harley 2003: 115)

> The 'memory' of a period of extreme weather may live in the minds of Welsh farmers for longer. Storytelling is an important part of Welsh culture, described as 'an organic part of the joy of everyday conversation.
> (Gwyndaf 1992: 225)

> Furthermore, a farmer's memory of everyday weather would be in stark contrast to that of an indoor city worker . . . [because of] a farmer's close proximity and dependency on the weather.
> (Jones et al. 2012: 43)

Water falling as rain, flooding the fields and running as waterfalls, springs and rivers is not only a frequent material occurrence, but also a constant source of discussion in, and when talking about, Wales. The amount of water that the country enjoys tends not to be coupled with long periods of sunny days and warm temperatures but instead is accompanied by many dark or grey days with low temperatures. As Wales has short growing seasons, long winter months and a relatively rocky highland landscape that is troubled by thin, poor, water-leached soils (Armstrong 2016), subsistence methodologies in its rural locations have historically favoured livestock farming (typically sheep) above other methods of subsistence (although Welsh recipes are also renowned for certain crops, such as leeks and their marine ingredients including oysters, mussels and laver seaweed on bread). While regular, slashing rain is to be expected through the winter months, (and is relied upon to produce the rich green grass for the sheep on the hills), consistent rainfall through the summer months causes recurring problems for farmers, by, for example, detrimentally affecting hay bailing, and rotting both the crops in the field and the wool on the backs of the sodden sheep. As a result, the agricultural communities in Wales have dutifully documented the weather in their farming diaries, as Macdonald et al. (2010) show to have been the case since as far back as the mid-1700s. Moreover, successfully surviving extreme weather occurrences during the winter months also illustratively supports the image of sturdy resilience and patience that Welsh farming communities employ (Jones et al. 2012). Heavy snowfall and the floods that can follow are documented as having caused significant trouble for inhabitants living higher up the mountains and, similarly, lower down, in the valleys. Snow has sometimes even restricted movement for up to ten weeks at a time (Jones et al. 2012) as this account from 1875 demonstrates:

> I well remember the flood on August 12th 1875 due to a cloud burst on Tyucha and Cedig moors. So terrific was the force of the rain and hailstones that the shooters and keepers had to lay down faces downwards in the heather to escape the violence of the storm. The villagers heard the sound of rushing waters in the distance coming at a terrific rater down Coedyglyn. Fortunately for the Village the flood divided itself at Tyucha farm and opened out into the fields and lanes, this saving many lives in the Village. The gable end of the school was struck by the force of water and luckily fell outwards and the building was flooded . . . several cattle were drowned on this eventful day. Strange to note that my wife has a vivid and lively

recollection of the incident, as she was one of the children who were rescued from the school. The Cross Guns Inn was flooded and the barrels of beer were floating about the Village.
(Jones, n.d., cited in Rowlands 2005: 15)

In more contemporary times, water remains something of a threat. In 2016, newspapers reported that the residents of the village of Eglwyswrw in Pembrokeshire had suffered eighty-five days of rain without respite (Cooper 2016), rivalling the record of eighty-nine days of rain recorded in Scotland in 1923 (Cooper 2016). According to reports, the locals experienced rain each day from October 2015 until the end of January in the following year. The waterlogged land and the consequences for farmers living in rural locations, as well as the psychological effects of incessant rain, should not be underestimated, even in a country in which rain is expected. In association, reports state that the amount of rainfall and extreme weather events are set to rise as a consequence of climate change (IPCC 2007).

However, the locals do not just despair about the weather that they live with; they also laugh about the amount of water that rains down on them each year.

> In the Bible, God made it rain for forty days and forty nights. That's a pretty good summer for Wales. That's a hosepipe ban waiting to happen. I was eight before I realised you could take a cagoule off.
> (Rhod Gilbert, Welsh comedian, 2012)

Comedy aside, Wales's reputation for having a lot of water is also promoted by the locals themselves. From diverse discussions with inhabitants, the locals consider themselves lucky to be living in a country that is abundant with water, despite its destructive abilities. The sufficiency of the supply is evident in the rich – almost shining – green of the hills as much as it presents in the low-hanging, gloomy grey skies that regularly threaten the lowlands and the rounded peaks of the mountains that run across the country. Consequently, (similarly to the false stereotype that Inuit communities have multiple words for snow) rain (*glaw*) is not presented as just one thing in Wales. As this piece from *The Guardian* illustrates, rain pervades Welsh thinking and so is present in the language:

What is perhaps most surprising is that most of them are single descriptive words for almost all states of precipitation from drizzle to pouring and worse. Although there are words for 'spotting', 'big spaced drops', 'short sharp showers', it is for the more serious rain that the language comes into its own. So there are different single words that translate as 'pouring very quickly', 'throwing it down' and 'fierce rain.'

Moving up a gear at least in the quantity of water coming down there are additional single words that mean 'sheets of rain', 'fountain rain', 'beating rain', 'bucketing rain' and 'maximum intensity rain'. The Welsh also have descriptive phrases. The English 'It is raining cats and dogs' has the equally baffling but perhaps more colourful Welsh equivalent 'It's raining old women and sticks'.

(Brown 2011)

In addition, in conversation, I have been told that hail is translated in Welsh as 'hard rain' (Steve 2017 (pers. comm.)). Indeed, it is not unusual to feel rain when the sky is blue, experience the rain hitting sharp like pins in your face, or almost as sheets of horizontal water that, combined with the wind, push you across the Welsh countryside, effortlessly penetrating or infiltrating into everything. Consequently, this palpable assemblage of wetness is not just experienced; it is also reflected throughout Welshness. For example, many place names reflect Wales's wateriness, as Thomas Morgan is at pains to explain:

> A great number of our place-names describe graphically the physical features of the country. Mountains, hills, and mounds, rocks and cliffs, glens and combes, moors and woods, rivers and brooks, all contribute their quota to the treasury of our nomenclature ... Aber means the mouth of a river, a particular point at which the lesser water discharges itself into the greater. In the old Welsh it is spelt [sic] aper, and Professor Rhys, Oxford, derives it from the root ber, the Celtic equivalent of fer, in Lat. Fer-oe, Greek phero Œ English bear. It originally meant a volume of water which a river bears or brings into the sea, or into another river; but it is now generally used to denote an estuary, the mouth of a river.
>
> Ach is a Celtic derivative particle denoting water. Agh in Ireland means a ford, och signifies the same in Scotland, and the Latin

aqua has the same meaning. The Sanscrit ux, uks, means to water. We find many brooks and rivers called Clydach, sheltering water; Achddu means black water, amdgwyach is a general term for several species of water-fowl. Afon, a river, comes probably from the Celtic awon, the moving water. . . . It is found in English in the form of Avon, which, in the opinion of Professor Rhys, appears to have been entitled to a v as early as the time of Tacitus. This form occasions redundancy in the English language. To say 'Bristol is on the river Avon' is tantamount to saying 'Bristol is on the river river.' Afon, a common name, has become a proper name in England, but in Wales it is the generic term for a river.

(Morgan 1887: 2–4)

Notwithstanding some fairly dramatic regional variation, Welsh towns therefore tend to have a ready supply of water to feed their populations. Similarly, while it is becoming more common for UK citizens living in England to brace themselves for restrictions on water consumption due to predicted water shortages that are regularly expected during the summer months, the Welsh have not had to suffer any limitations. In 2006, and again in 2012 when the British Government considered a hosepipe ban in England, *Dŵr Cymru* managed to ensure that Welsh homes maintained their supplies throughout (BBC News 2006; WalesOnline 2012).

Discourses on deluge

As water flows effortlessly from the sky, down the slopes of the mountains and into the valleys, making its way through people's lives and back to the sea, in Wales there has been no need to focus much attention on its retention or redirection over the years. In contrast to the populations of drier areas of our planet such as Kenya or Spain, inhabitants of Wales have not had to be concerned about their access to water; it is a constant companion, swelling the rivers, pouring out of mountain springs and remaining as sticky muddy puddles deep into the summer months in shaded wooded areas.

However, water has not simply run through people's lives without concern. On the contrary, it is also experienced as threatening in volume. Here, water's material ability to submerge and abruptly produce new lakes has been noted as routinely causing dramatic changes to the Welsh landscape by reshaping and reclaiming land. Narratives that detail water's ability to repossess areas of territory abound, both mythologically and historically. For example, Dooge (1996) reveals the repetitive and recurring theme of water in Celtic mythology, in which, echoing modern conclusions about water molecules (see earlier and Ball 2002), water was understood and depicted as a knowledgeable material that had the influence and authority to reshape the world (Dooge 1996). Water was explained as the 'leakage of wisdom from the Otherworld to our human world' (Dooge 1996: 17) and was held to be prone to producing sudden dramatic 'lake-bursts' (Dooge 1996: 18) that possessed the power to drown and conceal towns without warning.

Dooge (1996) links the watery contents of Celtic myths to the climatic activities of the Bronze Age. Citing Markale (1976), he asserts that fluctuations in the climate during that time forced Celts to migrate further north and west as a result of intense flooding across the land masses that are now known as Europe. This, he claims, not only accounts for the multiple stories of submerged, buried and abandoned villages that are found in Celtic myths, but also indicates that they are based in material (or physical) realities and genuine events (Dooge 1996: 1).

Many of the lakes that currently occupy areas of Wales are colourfully associated with rich mythological stories that attribute water with a selection of moralistic and cleansing powers. Llyn y Fan Fach at Myddfai, Llyn Tegid at Bala, and Llyn Syfaddan in Powys are all bodies of water that are considered to be mythologically significant and formidable. Often, lakes are depicted as being capable of unusual and unexpected behaviour. For example, lakes in Wales can simply manifest overnight, without warning, and also have the ability and tendency to deluge and destroy towns in their formation. Thus, lakes do not simply rise up and cover land; water becomes lakes by (as it were) working together, by maintaining its collectivity and, through the force that it can exert when 'together', is able to take back or retain control over the landscape. Equally, each body of water is represented as having its own threatening powers. The water in Llyn y Fan Fach is said to be dark and bottomless, with a tendency to boil, but also contains a 'lady' or enchantress who is believed to emerge from a doorway to an underworld (Gwyndaf 1989). Llyn Syfaddan also hides a world, as it is the site of a drowned town that was flooded because of greed and misconduct; and similarly the waters of Llyn Tegid at Bala rose up and covered the town despite warnings that could have prevented it if they had been heeded (Gwyndaf 1989). Another such story concerns the dramatic and swift drowning of a town in Porthcawl, Bridgend in Glamorgan, south Wales, to form the body of water that is now known as the Pool of Kenfig. Showing obvious correspondences with the examples above, legend has it that a castle lies buried in the sand that was dramatically blown in from the sea to cover it, and that a town also lies beneath the lake that formed after the sand had blown in. In repetition of similar themes outlined above, both town and castle were submerged by a storm as vengeance for forbidden activities – this time, a socially unacceptable marriage.

Additionally, the deluge myth of *Cantre'r Gwaelod* is sometimes called the Welsh Atlantis story, as it tells of a parcel of land that has now disappeared following a rapid flood. Previously the home to sixteen different kingdoms (at some undefined point in history), it is also depicted as having been drowned as a result of the morally contemptuous activities of drunkenness and forgetfulness. Now, any debauched revelries that may have taken place in this region lie submerged and silenced under the water of Cardigan Bay (the expanse of water located between and linking the mainlands of Wales and Ireland).

As with many mythical stories, the land in *Cantre'r Gwaelod* is said to have been exceptionally fertile and, if visible, the inundated palaces would reflect its previous abundance (see the overview of the Giriama creation myth in Chapter 5). That it was flooded meant that a decadent world was destroyed. This narrative continues the recurring themes recounted above, and adds to the numerous accounts that illustrate how the material behaviours of water impact on both the physical and cultural landscape of the Welsh.

Of equal interest to the multiple deluge legends is Bryant and Haslett's remarkable claim (2003, 2007) that Wales suffered a tsunami in the early 1600s. Taking various anecdotal but documented descriptions of the storm of 1607 alongside the archaeological, geological and morphological signs left in the landscape, Bryant and Haslett assert that, together, they support the notion that this was not just a storm but a tsunami, with waves of water measuring over 6 metres high hitting the landscape. This event spectacularly flooded the southwestern corner of Britain (including most of south Wales), and, they claim, killed over 2,000 people (Bryant and Haslett 2007). Flooding in the Severn Estuary and the nearby Bristol Channel is unexceptional, but accounts from the time demonstrate that this 'storm' was quite different in strength and ability from others – as is illustrated by the following passage from Morgan (1882), cited by Bryant and Haslett (2003):

> The Severn Sea after spring tide being driven back by a strong south-west wind that blew three days without intermission, rose to such a height with a most violent sea wind that the swell broke in upon the low ground ... with the greatest violence.
> (Morgan 1882: 3)
>
> Affirmed to have runne . . . with a swiftness so incredible, as that no gray-hounde could have escaped by running before them.
> (Morgan 1882: 4 cited by Bryant and Haslett 2003: 164)

From the accounts offered so far, it is clear that the overwhelming force of water to regularly take back land through submersion has conceptually and materially confronted the people of Wales throughout history. An excess of water on agricultural land has been a regular threat to subsistence across Britain. According to Trafford (1970), 12 million acres of land was underdrained in Britain and Wales by the middle of the twentieth century, to support successful agriculture. However, draining land is a costly business and benefits lowlands, such as the agricultural areas of east England, significantly more than high or upland areas, such as Wales. Consequently, most Welsh tenants, who were at the mercy of landowners, were unlikely to instal drainage because of the costs and reduced benefit, and therefore had to negotiate flooding on a regular basis. In contrast with previous geographical and cultural examples in which water is repeatedly sought, coaxed and negotiated with, in Wales, water exerts influence through its ability to reshape and alter the landscape rapidly – seemingly even overnight – through its ability to collect and failure to seep into the already saturated clay soils. Nevertheless, as in other locations, water adopts the character of both provider and bully, determining possibilities and redefining futures – a characterization that, one might hazard a guess, could manifest more obviously across the world at this point in the Age of the Anthropocene.

Water relationships, powers and control

Historically, the relationship between the Welsh and their neighbours, the English, has been fraught (Thomas 2013). One could argue that this is evident in the terms – 'Welsh' and 'Wales' – that are used by the English to describe the people and the country. Both words are Germanic in origin and mean 'foreigner' in English – something that one can understand might not be appreciated by the locals. The word used in Wales to describe the country and national identity is '*Cymru*', meaning 'fellow country man' or 'land of friends' (Griffiths 2007) – a term that makes no reference to any boundaries or the neighbouring country but demonstrates a sense of camaraderie and acknowledgement of sameness. Much has been written about the tensions between Wales and England, particularly in association with England competing to take over Welsh land and resources (Thomas 2013). This is so much so that I do not need to go into any detail here: suffice to say that historically – and for some, currently – a friction exists between nations, with the Welsh contesting the submergence of their culture and asserting their rights for their nationality, language and governance to be realized and revitalized. England's shameful imperial and colonial past still casts a long shadow over many parts of the world, including Wales. My aim here is not to produce a historical timeline of events but rather to demonstrate the role that water has had to play in shaping Welsh national identity, specifically while in relationship with the English, and as a consequence of England's designs on Welsh water.

Notwithstanding (or, perhaps, because of) the obvious abundance of water in this relatively small country, its value as an economic resource was not earnestly exploited before the Industrial Revolution, and this exploitation came in association with a combination of changing social, political and economic needs and conceptions of water. Water, particularly as steam, emerged as a key driver that powered technological developments across the world, not only by servicing the textile (and other) mills in various ways, but also through its role in transportation and the invention of the engine. During this March of Progress (also known as the March of Mind), steam figured highly and is responsible for the notion and fashion (or style) of 'steampunk' today (Ashley 2014; see also Attala 2018).

As in other parts of the global north, the 1800s was a time of unprecedented economic and social change in Britain. This occurred with the 'invention' and promotion of new ways of living that drew people away from working on the land in rural locations and towards the enticements of modernity and the purported security of wage labour in urban settings (Engels 2010). This move, cited as the foundational activity and launch of the Age of the Anthropocene, was generated by the production and encouragement of novelty, and the notion of progression with regard to chemistry, biology and engineering (Latour 1993b). Water's materiality, and the resultant technology that it enabled, played a significant part in the efficacy and inception of industrialization, and, indeed, without water's material behaviours, industry could not have developed in the way that it has (Attala 2018). Thus the burgeoning of industry, and the consequential dramatic increase in the population of an attentive, locally available workforce that it necessitated, is easily illustrated by the following:

> In 1801, about 20% of the population lived in towns over 5000. This increased to 55% by 1851 and 77% by 1911 ... by 1851 there were ten towns with over 100,000 people ... West Midlands was one of the main conurbations of 1,500,000.
>
> (Nagle 1998: 22)

However, the demand for an increased supply of water was not only economically instigated. Multiple impacting consequences played a part in this, including the bio-social effects of this revolution (cf. Latour 1993b). As English urban conurbations and industries expanded exponentially, epidemics of diseases such as typhus, cholera, tuberculosis and pneumonia did, too. As any connection between waste, germs and disease was yet to be made (Pasteur's Germ Theory was proposed in 1867), disease transmission was commonly thought to occur through the miasmic spread of poisonous air, and therefore had little to do with hygiene. Without recourse to evoke change to support improvements in their social and employment conditions, and as deadly epidemics swiftly mounted in frequency, populations began to riot. Liverpool suffered one of the worst of these so-called 'cholera riots' in 1832, causing a cascade of consequences that culminated in the recognition that a clean water supply was needed to protect the population. In 1842, Chadwick's 'Report on the Sanitary Conditions of the Laboring Population of Great Britain' called for, and then heralded, a series of changes to create what was advertised as a physically and morally cleaner Britain, which needed more water.

Memories of floods and flooding

The water that was essential to drive the rapidly developing industrial processes in England's cities was not sufficiently available in surrounding rivers. This problem demanded an immediate solution, without which production would be impacted. The solution: to source proximal water supplies, to inhibit water's journey to the sea, to construct vast reservoirs with a view to damming and holding on to the water and thereby piping the necessary fluid trapped in the dams into the cities that needed it. Initial solutions meant that dams were constructed locally (that is, for example, in Liverpool's hinterland). Unfortunately, however, the reservoirs rapidly became incapable of meeting the mounting hydro needs of such dramatically emerging urban communities, which led the British Government to consider appropriating areas in north Wales as potential sites for reservoirs. Reservoirs in Wales could easily fill and therefore would successfully quench the growing thirst of the Midlands. Being topographically higher, with water-rich valleys and relatively close to the Midlands permitted Welsh water to be deemed an effective choice for a gravity-fed system to communicate water (and in some instances coal and timber) across distances, using canal boats that moved along skilfully engineered aqueducts. In 1880, therefore, after preliminary investigations but few discussions with the locals (Thomas 2013), Liverpool was given Royal Assent to construct a reservoir and aqueduct system to dam up, and then draw from, Welsh water so as to provide English cities (via Oswestry treatment works) with what it required. It was this Royal Assent that produced Lake Vyrnwy – the first reservoir in Wales, designed specifically to benefit English industry over the border (Rowlands 2005: 1). The lake was completed in 1888 and at the time was the largest human-made dam in Europe, with a wall 100 feet high (Thomas 2013). The water had to travel 68 miles to Liverpool (Thomas 2013).

> A lake will come on Llanwddyn, to drown
> All the drunkards in the valley
> I wonder whether Rhysyn will be drowned
> Together with his goose-iron, in his own
> District, quite dazed.
>
> (Rowlands 2005: 15)

The poem above (echoing the sentiments of some of the mythical stories recounted earlier) presciently describes the events that were to redefine the shape and materiality of the Welsh village of Llanwddyn some years later. Rowlands (2005), quoting heavily from the records of a local policeman named David Jones, offers us descriptions of both village life and the monumental events that culminated in the flooding of the valley and drowning of Llanwddyn approximately ten years later in 1889 (Rowlands 2005). According to Jones, the word 'Vyrnwy' that was chosen to name the reservoir derives from the phrase 'the land of eight rivers' (Rowlands 2005: 4) – a name that offers us insight into the value and significance of the water and the rivers in that valley. In addition, the following passage illustrates further materio-cultural entanglements and the overall pervasiveness of the watery agency in this location.

> The calm and peaceful little hamlet had its church and two chapels and about thirty seven inhabited houses, all are now under seventy feet of water. The river Cedig had, in course of ages, brought down from the mountains an accumulation of stone and gravel and, on this, the old village was built. Most of the houses were built of river stones and, in some case, mud was used as mortar. The poorer houses were paved with cobble stones in the most antiquated manner.
>
> (Jones n.d., cited by Rowlands 2005: 6)

In addition, getting to the village was both impeded and mediated through and with water, as this description of the journey by postman Robert Jones illustrates:

> Our old friend had trudged the roads for upwards of twenty years between Llanfyllin and Llanwddyn, up one day and down the next calling at Llanfihangel on the way and in those days he had to face many difficulties . . . [there were] no less than three rivers to ford that were often in flood, which he bravely faced. The bridges were only built in 1881.
>
> (Jones n.d., cited by Rowlands 2005: 8)

Not only was water evident through the weather and the confluence of rivers running from the higher ground; the resonance of water was ever present for the locals to hear: 'the distant sound of the Ceunant-y-Pistyll Waterfall that often rang in our ears' (Jones n.d., cited by Rowlands 2005: 7).

While the scheme to build a reservoir over the village produced local anxieties about loss of their land, the population were financially compensated, thus paving the way for similar projects in the future (Rowlands 2005).

Before flooding the valley with water, the area was flooded with incomers – navvies – seeking work; the decade-long construction was once described as the 'ten years of plenty in the valley' (Rowlands 2005: 17). Building the reservoir was recognized as an extraordinary feat of engineering and, from accounts, it appears that the locals also found some wonder in its construction (Rowlands 2005). Indeed, building of this reservoir was fuelled both with the excited fervour of modernization that brought further technological advances right across Victorian Britain, as much as the need for the water that expansion demanded. Coopey and Tvedt (2006) are not alone in their suggestion that water projects epitomize modernity and that projects that cite progress as their intention trump the right of use above other rights. Moreover, in defence of the methods of development and developing, they state that: 'The key weapon in the armoury of the engineer . . . [and] the industrialised world was that of the notion of 'progress'" (Coopey and Tvedt 2006: xiv).

Consequently, its construction heralded a series of significant additional changes to human–environmental relationships and terms of engagement, along with a blending of national borders. Not only did the inhabitants have to move out of the valley to make way for the dam; workers also moved in, followed shortly afterwards by a selection of trades, goods and services necessary for their needs. Migration into Wales therefore also supported migration out of the valley that was being flooded, and even out of Wales, as numerous young Welsh moved out of the wet hills and into the drier urban locations to the north, in search of alternatives (Jones 2017). In other words, as the water began to course into England, shifts in other economic flows began to manifest and both communities and the shape of the landscape changed as a consequence.

After Llanwddyn was successfully drowned, further valleys inevitably followed. First came four reservoirs or lakes in the Elan Valley (built between 1893 and 1906), followed by another lake constructed between 1946 and 1952, which attracted a small amount of protest from militants who objected to the opening by Queen Elizabeth 'by blocking the route with a half-ton granite boulder blasted form the rock above the road' (Thomas 2013: 398). The construction of Elan Valley reservoirs also initiated the construction of the Pontcysyllte aqueduct that both delivers water to Liverpool and uses the travelling water to deliver coal on barges. Directly translated, 'Pontcysyllte' means 'the bridge that connects the river' and, since 1999, it has been recognized as a United Nations Educational, Scientific and Cultural Organization (UNESCO) World Heritage Site. In the 1960s, Capel Celyn was submerged in the Tryweryn Valley to produce Llyn Celyn – again to bring even more Welsh water to Liverpool (Casgliad y Werin Cymru n.d.).

According to Steve (a man in his sixties whose extended family has always lived in mid-Wales) the English were:

> The enemy we despised for many years. The English represented colonial arrogance and an Etonian approach. They made decisions about others' lands. Before, every acre was of huge importance to sustaining families. Now it's worthless because you can't make a living from it.
> (Steve 2017 (pers. comm.))

The following quote from Phil Bennett, a Welsh rugby player talking to the team before a match against England in 1978, offers further insight into how the Welsh felt about the English in Wales, and supports Steve's sentiment:

> Look at what these bastards have done to Wales. They've taken our coal, our water, our steel. They buy our houses and only live in them for a fortnight every year. What have they given us? Absolutely nothing. We've been exploited, raped, controlled and punished by the English and that's who you're playing this afternoon.
>
> (Bennett 1977, cited by Tibballs 2010: 218)

For Steve, and seemingly Bennett, English activity in Wales needs contestation. In our conversation Steve also remembered Dolgarrog as being illustrative of the unquestionable arrogance already mentioned above. In 1925, Dolgarrog suffered when two dams built to support its thriving aluminium industry failed, probably due to poor construction. The disastrous incident killed sixteen people when the dam burst and the forceful water surged through and smashed people's homes. Steve likens it to a lesser-known version of the more notorious Welsh disaster of Aberfan (in 1966), in which loose mounds of debris from the coal industry slipped as a result of water causing tip instability (Davies 1967). The huge piles of spoil surrounding the mining sites dominated the landscape around the pits. In hindsight, it is alarming to imagine that, in a country with as much rainfall as Wales, people were unconcerned about the mobility of the piles, especially as accounts show that locals expressed concern about the black, greasy water that was present (Davies 1967). On 21 October 1966, after normal but substantial rainfall – in an area that regularly experienced flooding – a subsiding pile dramatically and abruptly shifted due to the mound becoming 'liquified' (Davies 1967: 26). The slag buried the school and 116 of the town's children were killed under it – an event that Steve maintains should not have happened. Talking to Steve gives one a sense of both the anger and the weariness experienced by many in what they describe as the relentless struggle for the Welsh to be able to make their own decisions, to retain their national identity and stop feeling like victims of English choices. For Steve, this has little to do with water but it does have to do with *his* land in negotiation and the possibility of its being lost through being covered by water. The ability of water to silently remove the land from use is what both allowed the English to accumulate power and paradoxically supported the Welsh in collectively rising up against their oppressors. In this case, harnessing the water is the material factor that initially limited and restrained but, finally, enables the reappropriation of Welsh power.

Many of the political tensions that have been experienced between the English and the Welsh are inveigled in these examples, and demonstrate the material role that water has played in shaping relationships. The imperious attitudes embedded within the developmental intentions of the English alongside the aspirations of the Welsh reveal the contradictions and fundamental inequalities that are inherent in the association. On the one hand, employment opportunities increased and the receipt of wages or income made available through labour appeared to offer relative security to many. The chance to enhance living conditions in association with proposed developments presented what seemed to be a lucrative and beneficial climate for all concerned. However, for some, the price was problematic – simultaneously enchanting and sinister. For others, the price was also just too high – a sentiment that came to a head dramatically with the announcement of the intention to construct yet another reservoir for England in the Tryweryn Valley in the late 1950s (Thomas 2013).

Water and memory: 'Remember Tryweryn'

This section could be subtitled 'Welsh water fights back', but that could be accused of being somewhat misleading. However, in this section I aim to demonstrate how the material abilities, and the conclusions reached about water's capabilities (specifically its ability to drown and silence communities coupled with the force that it exerts when released after containment), are responsible for provoking the politically charged activities that ultimately began the process of shifting control of the water back to the Welsh from the English. Water's part in instigating or inspiring and then materializing this shift in power comes alongside attempts to divert water from its intended path. This was not so much to deprive Wales of its water – because there is plenty of it – but instead concerns redirection and appropriation without democratic process. Water as the epitome of democracy has force when in collective. Similarly, people, too, obtain and create power when they work collectively. On the surface of this example, the economic value of water appears to be the key factor, but it was not just its commercial worth that prompted the counter-activities that followed the construction of the reservoirs; it was the physical fact that the wateriness of Welshness was being contained and drained away to serve foreign purposes that acted as a precursor for what was to follow. That water is able to obscure, drown and muddy situations could be thought symbolically significant, but this was not the articulating force. Instead, it was the creation of structures designed to inhibit movement and control water that materially demonstrated the power that England was exercising over the landscape and excited the minds that went on to challenge the decision that the English imagined that they could make about Wales without consequence. By trapping the water, the locals experienced the oppression that was dissolved within the complexity of the situation and, as the amount of water in the reservoir accumulated, so did the force of feeling against those attempting to regulate the materiality of being Welsh. Water therefore acted as a partner in the fight against English control and, through its enslavement to English concerns, emphasized the material inequalities and injustice wrought over the Welsh.

During 1957, in another undertaking that demonstrated England's obvious and uncontested ability to trap, use and control Welsh water, by an Act of Parliament (issued in London) Liverpool Corporation was given the right to obstruct the River Tryweryn. In so doing the Corporation was permitted to drown the village of Capel Celyn and an area of the surrounding farmland – again, to provide water for those living over the border, at the expense of those living in Wales. Work began in 1960, after the last villagers were moved out and scattered across the country in different locations, thereby breaking the familial roots that, for generations, had so firmly embedded their lives to that part of the landscape.

According to anecdotes, Capel Celyn was one of the last villages populated entirely by Welsh speakers and, consequently, the decision about Welsh lives that had been made by the English, in England and without local consultation, was received with outrage, as might have been be expected (Thomas 2013). This plan would not only transform the land use to one that would benefit English businesses but, in doing so, would uproot the Welsh from both the land and use of the water. The process of disconnection from the materiality of Wales was anticipated as one that would detrimentally affect Welsh culture, history and livelihoods. This was the stance adopted to promote dissent.

In contrast to previous reservoir development schemes in Wales, the project that was designed to destroy the village of Capel Celyn came at a time when technological advances meant that communication methods had improved. These changes meant that many British families now had black-and-white televisions in the corners of their living rooms (Steve 2017). Consequently, the news of the plans to build a reservoir that was designed to span across the valley of Tryweryn were able to reach more people with greater speed than any of the previous plans for reservoirs that had been instigated by the English in Wales. Accordingly, the situation acted as 'a catalyst by nationalists to galvanize support for a flagging independence movement' (Coopey and Tvedt 2006: xxv). Using questions of water ownership as the foundation of the injustice and domination, a number of national independence groups were formed and, through them, support for the Welsh political party (Plaid Cymru) increased its membership substantially (Thomas 2013). A nationalist fervour boiled up and, like the water that was to fill the dam, collected and grew in strength. According to both Devine (2015) and Thomas (2013), Plaid Cymru doubled its membership after Tryweryn.

At the time that the Act of Parliament allowing the reservoir to be built was issued, thirty-seven Welsh members were able to vote in Parliament. Of that total, thirty-six voted against the proposal, but their votes were cast without effect and the Act conferring the right to drown the valley was passed, causing ordinary people to rise up and question the decision with both irritation and indignation. When the initial public protest against any construction was disregarded, public sentiment against the dam developed further and calls to stop the reservoir mounted, producing a number of unexpected consequences for some time. Just like the reverberations or ripples that are produced when a pebble drops into a body of water, the decision by Parliament spread opposition in ever-expanding concentric circles out from the point of contact for many years after the decision was made. Cumulatively, the initial activities encouraged further protests, which meant that, during the five years taken to build the reservoir, the construction process was regularly punctuated with public remonstrations, including two attacks of sabotage on the building works that caused activists to be imprisoned.

During the 1960s, various individuals moved to resist the decisions of the English and took it upon themselves to act against the building and smooth running of the reservoirs. The first incident in 1962 concerned two men, who, fired with a sense of injustice, travelled up from south Wales to release a thousand gallons of oil from the onsite transformer that generated the site's electricity. Their actions, designed with a view to drawing attention to the inherent discrimination of the acquisition by Liverpool of Welsh water and territory, began a timeline of media attention on what has been labelled 'Welsh terrorist' activities (Thomas 2013). This was the first blow to the English, and what followed were a number of minor terrorist activities, organized with increased frequency in a bid to sabotage and protest against the English colonial exploitation of Wales and Welsh lives. These actions aimed to 'send a clear message that the drowning of another Welsh valley would not be tolerated' (Thomas 2013: 39).

The formation of the *Mudiad Amddiffyn Cymru* (Movement for the Defence of Wales (MAC)) and, in 1963, the Free Wales Army (FWA) saw the beginning of organized bombings across Wales (Williams 2016). The FWA was formed in the small university town of Lampeter by less than a handful of young passionate men (one a student at the university), and led by William Cayo-Evans (known as 'Cayo'). The FWA claimed responsibility for a number of the attacks but is thought to have been responsible only for firing up attention through propaganda (despite its military-style uniforms and insignia) (Thomas 2013). According to Cayo's son, Rhodri, still living just outside Lampeter, on the road to Tregaron, his father was 'a really good terrorist' despite taking the leg off a passing child during bomb testing (InsaneMePlease 2010). The FWA's first appearance in public was in 1965, in the protest against the opening of the Llyn Celyn reservoir lake. Its first performance set its image in the public's mind as a group of active nationalist independence fighters. Its attempts to destroy or hinder progress on the reservoir meant that two of their number spent some time in jail, which became good advertising for their cause. Rather insensitively, or perhaps as a strategy by the Crown, only four years later, in 1969, the English decided to hold the investiture of Prince Charles as Prince of Wales at Caernarfon Castle. For the Welsh, however, Owain Glyn Dŵr (trans. 'Owen of the Glen of Dee Water' (Johnson. n.d.) – a name that references the water in the River Dee) is, in fact, the last rightful ruler of Wales (and native Prince of Wales), and the last Welsh man who successfully led a revolt against English rule in the 1400s. Fifty years on, the Facebook group 'Free Wales Army/Byddin Rhyddid Cymru Appreciation Society' has the following information pinned at the top of its page, which demonstrates that feelings from the past live on:

> His name will be verified by the generations of our people, to reclaim for him his nationhood. We will hail him, he who slumbers in the depth of eternity. Glyndwr was one of our greatest, and bravest in the sorrowful history of our princes. His spirit was aflame with patriotism. In his effort and sacrafice [sic], he fought against tremendous oods [sic], challenging the enemy, spilling their blood on the screaming fields where death found them. He had fire in his soul, gaurding [sic] our country's dignity from the most evil agtagnoists [sic] is the history of our nation. What a tremendous price to pay for freedom, losing his crown, his land and family. The foe merciless, reaping a harvest of revenge against a vanquished nation. His grave kept in secret for centuries in silence of lament. But, his name will not be forgotten, hidden away in the darkness of our saddened land. He armed his people in defence of our country, and his gallantry was prized and respected among the nations of Europe, pledging himself to free our nation from the shackles of serfdom. Let us commemorate his uprising, and pay him extreme tribute for such valour. His spirit is with us in solidarity. The shadow of time is creeping on, to save our people from extinction. Therefor [sic], let us pledge ourselves, in the name of a gallant prince, to honour our banner, our language, traditions and culture. And whosoever betrays our rights to freedom, may eternal contempt cover them.
>
> (Dennis Coslett, Machynlleth 14 September 2002)

The organization called MAC, on the other hand, now disbanded after its leader was imprisoned for ten years, orchestrated a more effective and menacing campaign that 'was responsible for many of the explosions' (Thomas 2013: x) and, according to Thomas, lay at the centre of aiding Wales 'to wake up to the grim truth that its essential cultural identity was at stake' (2013: xi).

The official opening of Llyn Celyn reservoir was hailed as a day of celebration, but was not experienced as such by the Welsh. Fuelled by the previous years of active but failed attempts to arrest the English plans, attendees made a final attempt to obstruct the proceedings through a selection of minor deeds of sabotage, such as stone throwing, cutting wires to the microphones and starting minor contretemps in the crowds. Collectively, these performances did little more than cause the atmosphere to become threatening but, nevertheless, as a result, the planned ceremony had to be abandoned. These years of impotent action allowed the powerlessness and inability of the Welsh to cause decisions about their country to bubble up to the surface, and the ensuing actions made this fact sharply felt across the country.

Until this point in history – despite various attempts to dislodge the English – the Welsh had remained unable to shift English authority out of their land. The following years' activities were instrumental in shifting this authority and producing the devolved Government of today. For historian Wyn Thomas, the events of 1965 present as a turning point for Wales and have since been recognized as a defining moment that succinctly symbolized the problems of the two countries' relationship (2013). Thomas – for some, controversially – links this humiliating event with the successive implementation of the Welsh Language Acts and the further establishment of the Welsh National Assembly Government in the 1990s, the Government of Wales Act in 2006, and the referendum in 2011 that finally gave Wales back the powers to 'control' its water. Consequently, using Thomas's ideas, one could claim that national feeling, previously lying somewhat dormant prior to the plans to construct the reservoir, were reawakened (or even revitalized) and then developed into the small but potent and coherent movement that affected the official opening day of the dam. Somewhat ironically, perhaps, but equally a testament to the people's inextricable connection to the material world of which they are part, it took what was depicted as the submersion of Welshness to act as a stimulus for the Welsh to push back against (what were locally conceived of as) the oppressors (Williams 2016).

The drowning of the village displaced forty-eight Welsh villagers with millions of litres of Welsh water, redirected with a view to supplying the English with their hydro needs. This began a process that helped to transform the Anglo-Welsh affiliation and return powers of governance to Wales. Local descriptions of the moment of the event of flooding are poetic and poignant. They illustrate people's deep sense of loss that was engendered as the water rushed in to take their homes away.

> I remember the water coming out in a huge gush. There was nothing left – not a tree, a hedge, no sheep, cattle, or birds singing. It was deathly quiet like a funeral ... we lost our heritage; we lost everything.
>
> (Elwyn Edwards, aged 67, cited in Richards 2010)

The sense of a deathly silence falling over the valley, as described above by Elwyn, was a temporary physical consequence of the moment. As the land was covered and detained under the water, however, Welsh voices were far from silenced. Indeed, the filling of another reservoir did not drown out Welsh voices at all. On the contrary, rather than being further buried or submerged under the water, Welshness rose up louder as the walls of the construction trapped and held the water within its confines. Effectively imprisoned and redirected in its purpose, the water symbolically spoke through the people with whom it would otherwise have engaged, and physically reflected and embodied the strength of collectivity. Consequently, these events also illustrate another way in which water is able to simultaneously (physically and politically) shape our lives.

During October 1965, the words '*Cofiwch Dryweryn*' ('Remember Tryweryn') appeared painted on the side of a derelict building that backs on to a wide bend on the A487 near Llanrhystud, Aberystwyth. The slogan was accompanied by the FWA symbol, both of which were brandished in red and white paint, and stand over 10 feet tall. Its appearance was a local response to the outcry prompted by the drowning of Capel Celyn, and is written on the location said to be the centre of Owain Glyndŵr's true kingdom (Rosemary 2017 (pers. comm.)). Meic Stephens, a prolific author and nationalist, was responsible for the original act of graffiti. He describes the slogan as his 'most famous statement, my best-known poem, my most eloquent speech, and my most influential political act' (Stephens, cited by Osmond 2009). Now his nationalist protest graffiti slogan is held to be iconic and has assumed the status of a national landmark and monument with support from Cadw, the Welsh Assembly and voluntary donations for its upkeep. 'In a leaflet promoting the fund-raising campaign Llanrhystud Council observes, "The flooding of the valley became a turning point in the history of Wales, convincing Welsh people that they must have the right to govern their own affairs'" (Osmond 2009). It is now an integral part of the fight to restore Welsh identity and symbolically represents the struggle that the Welsh have undergone (and are still undergoing) to regain their nationality and divorce themselves from the English cultural identity that has permeated theirs after the water was corralled and diverted out. These are 'the matters of Wales' (Davis 1993: 68) that remind us of the tangled material relationships that produce us, as the following example of Welsh poetry demonstrates.

Reservoirs

A poem by R. S. Thomas, originally published in 1968 not long after the flooding of Capel Celyn

> There are places in Wales I don't go:
> Reservoirs that are the subconscious
> Of a people, troubled far down
> with gravestones, chapels, villages even:
> The serenity of their expression
> Revolts me, it is a pose
> for strangers, a watercolour's appeal
> To the mass, instead of the poem's
> Harsher conditions. There are the hills
> Too; gardens under the scum
> Of the forests, and the smashed faces
> Of the farms with the stone trickle
> Of their tears down the hills' side.
>
> Where can I go, then, from the smell
> Of decay, from the putrefying of a dead
> Nation? I have walked the shore
> For an hour and seen the English
> Scavenging among the remains
> Of our culture, covering the sand
> Like the tide and, with the roughness
> Of the tide, elbowing our language
> Into the grave that we have dug for it.
> (Thomas 2000: 194)

Yma o hyd (Still here)

Yma o hyd is the title of a song written by Dafydd Iwan in 1981. Some consider it the second national anthem of Wales:

> Ry'n ni yma o hyd, er gwaetha pawb a phopeth
> (We're still here, in spite of everyone and everything)
> (Wyn James 2005)

With this example, it is possible to see that the control of water should not be underestimated in its material and political effect. The processes that are necessary to dam water are complex and can produce unintended consequences, as can water's material abilities to cover, saturate, inundate, drown and engulf. Rather than land or the soil being of nationalist significance, this ethnographic example demonstrates that the relationships enacted in association with the material abilities of water produced an answer to the dissolution of Welsh national identity. As has already been made abundantly clear, water is able to co-produce multiple reactions and outcomes as it seeps into all aspects of life. While the 'control of water has, in many places and moments of history, been equated with the control of society' (Coopey and Tvedt 2006: x), this example illustrates how it is nothing less than the very materiality – the physical abilities – of water that has the power to contest and subvert this androcentric assertion. Rather than considering how water is (or has been) controlled for use, the adoption of an NM perspective encourages one to think about how the material behaviours of water actively shape the situation. It is undoubtedly the case that the physical abilities of water supported the development of certain mechanization technologies. Water's part in what Coopey and Tvedt term 'the industrialization of water' (2006: xviii), rather than the Industrial Revolution, therefore, must be acknowledged. Recognition of the role that water played in generating and harnessing new forms of power, as well as shaping other aspects of industrial lives (for example, meeting the newly realized hygiene needs of the rapidly increasing populations that were living and accumulating in developing urban settings such as Birmingham and Liverpool), supports recognition of the co-productivity of material relationships. Water's role in supporting these developments is not incidental, and therefore should not be underestimated; without water's abilities, many of the advances simply could not have occurred as they have (Attala 2018). Consequently, to document these events as proceedings that categorize human interests or the use of resources as its primary lens relies on a human exceptionalist focus that ignores or sidesteps the formative relationships held between people and the other materials with which they engage in the creation of our shared worlds. In short, if water behaved other than it does, none of this would have happened as it did.

From the brief descriptions above, it is possible to imagine the amount of water to which the Welsh relate on a daily basis, and how Welsh identity is governed by water's behaviours. By looking at what happens when a profusion or abundance of water physically accumulates, it is possible to realize the material power of retained water. Water as a collective comprises and contains substantial power – enough to be able to exert sufficient physical force on the other materials with which it is in relationship. By directly paying attention to how water behaves *en masse*, as it were, allows us to understand the role that water's materiality has played in reminding the Welsh of their power, thereby creating a pathway towards revitalizing contemporary Welsh national identity. In this case, recognition of how water is able to saturate the soil; inundate and engulf areas; how, through saturation, it is able to linger, puddle, overwhelm and disrupt geographies; and how, in abundance, it can be redirected, restricted, inhibited, corralled and barricaded has been shown not only to represent power but to furnish those in relationship with it with certain powers.

Further attention to the mobility of water – specifically its ability to gush through valleys and flood the land – offers us both a material model and a metaphor by which to understand past political struggles and current political structures in Wales. The power of water to shape both social and physical landscapes is unmistakably apparent in this example. But, by way of reminder, our aim here is not simply to show that water is able to embody symbolic meanings or that it can exert influences over behaviours but that, in relationship, water and people co-produce each other in the ways made possible in that time and place. Thus, this example illustrates how water is a co-creative material actant in the formation of contemporary Welshness, alongside playing a part in contributing to the creation of English identities in Wales. Water's part in this is integral and therefore should not be thought of as incidental. Here, as was also seen in Chapter 5, which detailed water struggles in rural Kenya, it is both the weight of water and the fact that water was captured – even tamed and ultimately redirected, making it 'out of place' (to borrow Douglas's phrase (1966)) – that altered and shaped people's lives irrevocably. This is not because of the weight of carrying the water (as we saw previously) but because of the collective weight of and political consequences of water's ability to subsume land, villages and cultures.

As we have seen, water's ability to cover the land enables it to conceal or obscure from view what it is covering. By burying entities below and/or within it, the submerged entities subsumed under the water are held in fluid suspension: neither here nor there, and present but also simultaneously gone, as though held in a time without time – a cold, still and quiet world under the flood waters. However, water's transparency and tendency to alter its levels through various processes means that it cannot hide its plunder forever. Its clarity belies its actions. Thus, the manner by which water can flood and submerge is a material propensity that can be used to acquire and validate dominance (McCully 2001). When conceived in this way, it is water's materiality that transforms it into a politically charged tool. Moreover, using an NM perspective, what is presented as engineering materials (resources) emerges as a series of contested relationships circulating the materials that people live *with*. Consequently, flooding the valleys to support the needs of English towns and businesses did more than simply harness a resource, or symbolically reinforce England's dominance over Wales; it used the material abilities of water to expose the value of Welshness held by the colonial mindset of the English at that time, and to remind the Welsh of their collective powers. Put another way, if water were unable to behave in this way – if it were not a material that could subsume landscapes and drown items in its path – the English would not have been able to contain, redistribute and drain a core substance that forms the material heart of Wales. By destroying one village, in particular, through the creation and implementation of a reservoir in its place, Welsh water transformed from the lively vibrant actant that produced the bright green of Welsh hills to a heavyweight political shaper. As the waters rose in English-constructed dams, so rose the Welsh nationalist movement that has disrupted and challenged English rule in Wales.

This example illustrates how the material fact that water can be captured, contained and redirected away from an area alters the eco-materiality of space and places, and in turn reshapes relationships across the material spectrum. In this case, it is not just that water is redirected away and across the border from Wales into England that is of concern, but that the material connections between people and the world around them were significantly redesigned as a result of water's ability to be seized and redirected for purposes other than those previously manifest. An NM perspective offers a view on how the consequences of materials' abilities are active factors that co-productively (with people) shape outcomes.

8 CONCLUDING REMARKS

The New Materialities (NM) approach rejects a pointed focus on separate entities in favour of exploring the matter of relationships. It relates to relationships materially rather than by considering how objects influence each other through their existence. Presented through an NM lens, it is possible to note that both human and water's abilities are inextricably physically connected, and therefore undoubtedly inform or affect each other. Consequently, neither human nor water simply exists without reference to each other but instead existswith (following Haraway 2008) and therefore each mobilizes the other in different ways. Water impacts on how people can live, just as people alter the manner by which water flows, because both are constantly in existentially shaping relationship with each other. The purpose of this perspective is to represent the material reality formulating our lives and to discard once and for all the human exceptionalist approaches that frame people and what they make and do as elevated from the rest of the world's entities.

This book initially allowed the reader to become familiar with some of water's predilections, tendencies and devices, to create a picture of the dynamic physical techniques water can employ, and which, once manifest, go on to shape lives. Presenting an overview of water in this way was not designed to perpetuate notions of water's distinct materiality, but was constructed to explore what water urges doing in the field of living materials regardless of any connection to the assemblage of materials that we call 'people'.

By articulating a relational ontology, behaviours can be seen to impact on behaviours – not through the simplistic lens of cause and effect that relies on reductionist methods for conclusions but in a messy, complexity contingent on circumstances. Consequently, it follows that human activity is not exclusively reliant on biological drives, impulses or reasoned choices, as is often peddled, but results from the materiality (or blending of materials) that is inherent to being alive. In association, water is more than just an influencing factor that is available to be organized by people; it is a partner that exerts control over relationships and any designs. Therefore, the method, trajectory and process of any relationship are not primarily cognitive ones instigated by the mind but depend on engaging materialities (Ingold 2013). Relationships therefore create co-generative and co-productive performances, because of the way in which the engaging parties are able to relate to each other in the given conditions. In sum, how people can be with water is predicated on the way in which water behaves, or the physics of water's materiality, as much as people's ideas or their desires with regard to what they might want from water. Similarly, water shapes how people think about it, but this should not be mistakenly attributed to a symbolic association or conception. On the contrary, this directly concerns what water actually does to bodies and landscapes. As Strang (2015) reminds us, we literally think with water.

The three ethnographic examples presented here offer distinctive illustrations of how variable water–human relationships can be in different geographical and political contexts. In Kenya, people's bodies are sculpted by the arduous task of daily water haulage and the difficulties associated with seeking out water's hiding place when it is scarce. In addition, this example demonstrates how water's influence does not lie with biology or corporeality exclusively, but reveals how the material behaviours that water displays directly inform Giriama cultural ideas about identity, social expectations and ritual practices.

Similarly, in Spain, the mineral waters of Lanjaron co-create the town's identity through its material healing properties and its material ability to soak into the land, as it is gently coaxed across the otherwise desiccated terraces. The performance of a water festival that inundates the town with water over one night occurs because of water's ability to be stored when it is frozen and to melt in the summer months. Just when one might imagine water reserves would need to be preserved, the water is released to avoid stocks becoming bloated with the potential to cause damage. Therefore, what appears to be a wasteful practice is a pragmatic one, based around the material abilities of water in relationship with people's lives.

In Wales, where water flows in such abundance that it regularly floods and drowns land, being-with (Haraway 2008) water emerges as a key component to being Welsh. The attempt to sever the connection between the Welsh and the water that flowed through their lives was shown to be responsible for reminding the Welsh of their intractable relationship with the water that was being moved across the border by the English. This realization was made possible by the fact that water can be constrained, held and redirected off the paths that it carves for itself. The ability to contain water results from water's materiality, as does its ability to build its power as its volume increases. That local powers increased as the volume of dammed water grew reminds us that *human activity is material* and is not distinct from the world around it.

REFERENCES

Abrams, D. 1996. *The Spell of the Sensuous: Perceptions and Language in a More-than-Human World*. New York: Vintage, Random House.

AGWA. 2018. The Policy and Practice of Climate Change: Climate Policy is Water Policy. *Alliance for Global Water Adaptation* [online]. Available at *http://alliance4water.org/policy/*.

Amelang, J. S. 2013. *Parallel Histories: Muslims and Jews in Inquisitorial Spain*. Louisiana State University Press.

Appadurai, A., and Breckenridge. C. A. 2009. Foreword. In, Mathur, A., and Da Cunha, D. *Soak: Mumbai in an Estuary*. Rupa & Co: New Delhi, pp. 1–3.

Armstrong, E. 2016. *Research Briefing: Farming Sector in Wales*. National Assembly for Wales Commission [online]. Available at *http://www.assembly.wales/research%20documents/16-053-farming-sector-in-wales/16-053-web-english2.pdf*.

Ashley, M. 2014. *Inventing the Future British Library* [online]. Available at *https://www.bl.uk/romantics-and-victorians/articles/inventing-the-future*.

Attala, L. 2016a. Bodies of Water: Exploring Water Flows in Rural Kenya. In *Exploring the Materiality of Food 'Stuffs': Transformations, Symbolic Consumption and Embodiment*. Steel, L., and Zinn, K. (eds), Oxon, New York: Routledge, pp. 79–100.

Attala, L. 2016b. 'Digesting 'Cryptid' Snakes: A Phenomenological Approach to the Mythic and Cosmogenetic Properties of Serpent Hallucinations'. In Hurn. S (ed.) *Cryptozoology: Cross Cultural Engagements with Mysterious Creatures*. Ashgate: London, pp. 218–37.

Attala, L. 2017. The Edibility Approach: Using Edibility to Explore Relationships, Plant Agency and the Porosity of Species' Boundaries. *Advances in Anthropology* 7, pp. 125–45.

Attala, L. 2018. Mind the Gap! Exploring the Gap Between Harmony and the Watery Materiality of Climate Change(s) in Rural Kenya. In Campion, N. *Harmony Papers*. Bath: Sophia Press.

Attala, L., and Steel, L. (eds) 2019. *Body Matters: Exploring the Materiality of the Body*. Cardiff: University of Wales Press.

Ball, P. 2002. *H$_2$O: The Biography of Water*. London: Orion Book.

Barad, K. 2003. Posthumanist Performativity: Toward an Understanding of How Matter Comes to Matter. *Signs: Journal of Women in Culture and Society* 28: 3, pp. 801–31.

Barad, K. 2007. *Meeting the Universe Halfway: Quantum Physics and the Entanglement of Matter and Meaning*. Durham, NC: Duke University Press Books.

Bartholomew, A. 2012. *Hidden Nature: the Startling Insights of Viktor Schauberger*. Edinburgh: Floris Books.

BBC News. 2006. Hosepipe Ban in Wales 'Unlikely' *BBC News Channel* [online]. Available at *http://news.bbc.co.uk/1/hi/wales/4842186.stm*.

Bear, C. 2011. Being Angelica? Exploring Individual Animal Geographies. *Area* 43, pp. 297–304.

Bear, C., and Eden, S. 2011. Thinking like a Fish? Engaging with Nonhuman Difference Through Recreational Angling. *Environment and Planning D: Society and Space* 29: 2, pp. 336–52.

Beaucave-Gauvreau, E., Dumas, G. A., and Lawani, M. 2011. Head Load Carriage and Pregnancy in West Africa. *Clinical Biomechanics* 26: 9, pp. 889–94 [online]. Available at *http://www.sciencedirect.com/science/journal/02680033/26/9*.

Bennett, J. 2010. *Vibrant Matter: a Political Ecology of Things*. Durham and London: Duke University Press.

Bennett, P. 1977 cited by Tibballs, G. 2010. *The Bowler's Holding, the Batsman's Willey: The Greatest Collection of Humorous Sporting Quotations Ever!* Chester: Ebury Press.

Benveniste, J. 2017. Memory of Water. In *Essence of Water* [online]. Available at *http://essenceofwater.org/memory-of-water/*.

Blatter, J., and Ingram, H. (eds) 2001. *Reflections on Water: New Approaches to Transboundary Conflicts and Cooperation (American and Comparative Environmental Policy)*. Cambridge, MA; London: MIT Press.

Boivin, C. 2008. *Material Cultures, Material Minds: The Impact of Things on Human Thought, Society, and Evolution*. Cambridge: Cambridge University Press.

Boltz, F. 2017 in Rowling, M 2017. Thirsty World Must Wake up to Looming Water Crisis, Expert says. *Reuters* [online]. Available at

https://www.reuters.com/article/us-global-water-development/thirsty
-world-must-wake-up-to-looming-water-crisis-expert-says
-idUSKCN1B41V4.
Bowie, F. 2006. *The Anthropology of Religion: An Introduction*. Oxford: Blackwell.
Brantley, C. 1979. An Historical Perspective of the Giriama and Witchcraft Control. *Africa: Journal of the International African Institute*, 49: 2, pp. 112–33.
Brenan, G. 2008. *South From Granada*. Penguin Modern Classics, London: Penguin.
Brown, P. 2011. Weather Watch: the Many Welsh Words for Rain. *The Guardian* [online]. Available at https://www.theguardian.com/news/2011/aug/21/weatherwatch-wales-rain-drizzle.
Bryant, E. A., and Haslett, S. K. 2003. Was the AD 1607 Coastal Flooding Event in the Severn Estuary and Bristol Channel (UK) due to a Tsunami? *Archaeology in the Severn Estuary* 13, pp. 163–7.
Bryant, E. A., and Haslett, S. K. 2007. Catastrophic Wave Erosion, Bristol Channel, United Kingdom: Impact of Tsunami? *Journal of Geology* 115, pp. 253–69.
Candea, M., and Col da, G. 2012. The Return to Hospitality. *Journal of the Royal Anthropological Institute* 18: S, pp. 1–19 DOI: 10.1111/j.1467-9655.2012.01757.x.
Capra, F. 2002. *The Hidden Connections: A Science for Sustainable Living*. London: HarperCollins.
Capra, F., and Luisi, P. L. 2014. *The Systems View of Life: A Unifying Vision*. Cambridge: Cambridge University Press.
Carey, M. 2010. *In the Shadow of Melting Glaciers: Climate Change and Andean Society*. Oxford & New York: Oxford University Press.
Carse, A. 2010. Water. *Cultural Anthropology* [online]. Available at http://www.culanth.org/curated_collections/10-water.
Casgliad y Werin Cymru (The People's Collection Wales), n.d. *Reservoirs in Wales* [online]. Available at https://www.peoplescollection.wales/content/reservoirs-wales. Welsh Government Sponsored Site.
Cashmore, T. H. R. 1961. Tanganyika Notes and Records. *Journal of Tanganyika Society*. Dar es Salaam: Government Printer 57, pp. 153–72.
Cassidy, R. 2012. Lives With Others: Climate Change and Human-Animal Relations. *Annual Review of Anthropology* 41, pp. 21–36.

Castaing-Taylor, L., and Paravel, V. 2012. *Leviathan* [online]. Available at *http://www.arretetoncinema.org/leviathan/*.
Chadwick, E. 1842. *Report on the Sanitary Condition of the Labouring Population of Great Britain and on the Means of its Improvement* [online]. Available at *http://www.deltaomega.org/documents/ChadwickClassic.pdf*.
Charen, T. 1951. *The Etymology of Medicine* [online]. Available at *https://www.ncbi.nlm.nih.gov/pmc/articles/PMC195119/pdf/mlab00237-0040.pdf*.
de Châtel, F. 2015. *Water Sheikhs and Dam Builders: Stories of People and Water in the Middle East*. New York, Oxon: Routledge.
Chen, C. MacLeod, J., and Neimanis, A. 2013. *Thinking with Water*. Montreal and Kingston, London, Ithaca: McGill-Queen's University Press.
Clark, A., and Chalmers, D. 1998. The Extended Mind. *Analysis* 58: 1, pp. 7–10.
Coats, C. 2001. *Living Energies: Viktor Schauberger's Brilliant Work with Natural Energy Explained*. Dublin: Gill Books.
Cohen, J. J., and Duckert, L. 2015. *Elemental Ecocriticism: Thinking with Earth, Air, Water and Fire*. Minneapolis, London: University of Minnesota Press.
Consigli, P. 2008. *Water, Pure and Simple: The Infinite Wisdom of an Extraordinary Molecule*. London: Watkins Publishing.
Coole, D., and Frost, S. 2010. *New Materialisms: Ontology, Agency, and Politics*. Durham: Duke's University Press.
Cooper, J. 2016. Eglwyswrw Village Narrowly Misses Setting British Rain Record. *The Pembrokeshire Herald* [online]. Available at *https://pembrokeshire-herald.com/19463/eglwyswrw-village-narrowly-misses-setting-british-rain-record/*.
Coopey, R., and Tvedt, T. (eds) 2006. *A History of Water. Volume 2: The Political Economy of Water*. London: I.B. Tauris.
Coslett, D. 2002. *Free Wales Army / Byddin Rhyddid Cymru Appreciation Society* [online]. Available at *https://www.facebook.com/groups/2254866126/about/*.
Coxhead, N. 1985. *The Relevance of Bliss: a Contemporary Exploration of Mystic Experience*. London: Wildwood.
Cresswell, T. 2004. *Place: A Short Introduction*. Oxford: Blackwell.
Cruz, T. 2014. The Political Equator. In Mathur, A., and Da Cunha, D. (eds) *Design in the Terrain of Water*. California: Point Reyes Station.

Cuffey, K., and Patterson, M. 2010. *The Physics of Glaciers*, 4th edn. Oxford: Elsevier.

Daniel, E. Valentine. 1984. *Fluid Signs: Being a Person the Tamil Way*. Berkeley: University of California Press.

Davies, E. 1967. *Report of the Tribunal Appointed to Inquire into the Disaster at Aberfan on October 21st, 1966* pdf. London: Her Majesty's Stationery Office. OCLC.

Davies, R. 2016. Spain – Torrential Rain and Floods Leave 2 Dead *Floodlist* [online]. Available at http://floodlist.com/europe/spain-floods-costa-del-sol-december-2016.

Davis, W. V. (ed.) 1993. *Miraculous Simplicity: Essays on R. S. Thomas*. Fayetteville: University of Arkansas Press.

Derman, B., Odgaard, R., and Sjaastad, E. (eds) 2007. *Conflicts over Land and Water in Africa*. Suffolk: James Currey Publishers.

Derrida, J., and Dufourmantelle, A. 2000. *On Hospitality: Anne Dufourmantelle Invites Jacques Derrida to Respond* (Cultural Memory in the Present) (trans. Bowlby, R.). Stanford, California: Stanford University Press.

Descartes, R. 1985. *The Philosophical Writings of Descartes Vol. 1* (trans. Cottingham, J., Stoothoff, R., and Murdoch, D.). Cambridge: Cambridge University Press.

Descola, P. 2013. *Beyond Nature and Culture*. Chicago: Chicago University Press.

Devine, D. 2015. Tryweryn: Fifty Years on the Sense of Injustice is Still Raw – so What Happened, Why and What is the Legacy? *WalesOnline* [online]. Available at http://www.walesonline.co.uk/news/wales-news/tryweryn-fifty-years-sense-injustice-10300573.

Directorate-General for Research and Innovation. 2015. *Final report of the Horizon 2020 Expert Group on 'Nature-Based Solutions and Re-naturing Cities'*. EU Publications.

Dooge, C. I. 1996. Water and Celtic Mythology, Hydrologie dans les Paye Celtique, Rennes INRA (Les Colloques no 79). Centre for Water Research, University College Dublin. *Hydrologie.org* [online]. Available at http://hydrologie.org/ACT/CIC/CIC_1_013.pdf.

Douglas, M. 1966. *Purity and Danger: An Analysis of Concepts of Pollution and Taboo*. London: Routledge.

Dow, J. 1996. Ritual Prestation, Intermediate-level Social Organisation, and Sierra Otoni Oratory Groups. *Ethnology* 35: 3, pp. 195–202.

Drabu. O. 2017. The 44th Tribe: How Kenyan's Asians are Navigating the Upcoming Election. *Huffington Post* [online]. Available at https://www.huffingtonpost.in/2017/08/03/the-44th-tribe-how-kenyas-asians-are-navigating-the-upcoming-e_a_23062488/.

Drazin, A., and Küchler, S. 2015. *The Social Life of Materials: Studies in Materials and Society*. London, New Delhi, New York, Sydney: Bloomsbury.

Dundes, A. (ed.) 1981. *The Evil Eye: A Casebook*. London, Winconsin: The University of Wisconsin Press.

Durán Zuazo, V. H., Martínez, J. R. F., Tejero, I. C., Rodríguez Pleguezuelo, C. R., Martínez Raya, A., and Cuadros Tavira, S. 2012. Runoff and Sediment Yield from a Small Watershed in Southeastern Spain (Lanjarón): Implications for Water Quality. *Hydrological Sciences Journal*, 57: 8, pp. 1610–25.

Dŵr Cymru 2017. About Welsh Water: About Us. *Dŵr Cymru Welsh Water* [online]. Available at http://www.dwrcymru.com/en/Education/About-Welsh-Water.aspx.

Echarri, J., and Forriol, F. 2005. Influence of the Type of Load on the Cervical Spine: a Study on Congolese Bearers. *The Spine Journal* 5, pp. 291–6.

Edgeworth, M. 2011. *Fluid Pasts: Archeology of Flows (Debates in Archaeology)*. Bristol: Bristol Classical Press.

Edwards, E. 2010. Quoted in Richards, V. 2010. The Village Drowned to Give Another Nation Water. *Independent* [online]. Available at http://www.independent.co.uk/news/uk/this-britain/the-village-drowned-to-give-another-nation-water-2108977.html.

Empedocles in Leroi, A. M. 2014. *The Lagoon: How Aristotle Invented Science*. London, New York: Bloomsbury.

Engels, E. 2010. *The Origin of the Family, Private Property and the State*, trans. Hunt, T. London: Penguin Classics Reissue Edition.

ESRF.eu. 2010. Experimental Explanation of Supercooling: Why Water does not Freeze in Clouds. *European Synchrotron Radiation Facility* [online]. Available at http://www.esrf.eu/news/general-old/general-2010/supercooling.

Estevéz, M. 1864. Monografía de las Aguas y Baños Minero-Medicinales de Lanjarón, Madrid, Estab. Tipográfico de T. Fortanet. In Samos, J. P. 2006. El Agua Como Recurso Turístico en un Entorno Rural: el Balneario de Lanjarón in Eyzaguirre, F. M. (ed.) *Balnea:*

Establecimientos Balnearios: Historia, Literatura y Medicine. Anejo 1 Serie de Monografia, Publicaciones Universidad Complutense De Madrid.

European Commission. n.d. *Policy Topics (Environment): Nature Based Solutions* European Commission [online]. Available at *https:// ec.europa.eu/research/environment/index.cfm?pg=nbs*.

Eyzaguirre, F. M. 2006. The Figure of Medical Director in Lanjarón Spa: XIX century. In Eyzaguirre, F. M (ed.) *Balnea: Establecimientos Balnearios: Historia, Literatura y Medicine*. Anejo 1 Serie de Monografia, Publicaciones Universidad Complutense De Madrid.

Fagan, B. M. 2001. *The Little Ice Age: How Climate Made History, 1300–1850*. Basic Books.

Finney, J. T. 2004. Water? What's so Special About it? *Philosophical Transactions: Biological Sciences* Vol 3, The Molecular Basis of Life: Is Life Possible Without Water? 1448, pp. 1145–65.

Fishman, C. 2011. *The Big Thirst: The Secret Life and Turbulent Future of Water*. New York: Simon and Schuster.

Fontein, J. 2008. The Power of Water: Landscape, Water and the State in Southern and Eastern Africa: An Introduction. *Journal of Southern African Studies* 34: 4, pp. 737–56.

Fontein, J. (ed.) 2015. *Remaking Mutirikwi: Landscape, Water and Belonging in Southern Zimbabwe*. James Currey: East Africa Studies.

Friends of the Earth International. n.d. [online]. Available at *http://www.foei.org*.

Gandy, M. 2014. *The Fabric of Space: Water, Modernity, and the Urban Imagination*. Cambridge MA: MIT Press.

Geere, J. L., Hunder, P. R., and Jagals, P. 2010a. Domestic Water Carrying and its Implications for Health: A Review and Mixed Methods Pilot Study in Limpopo Province, South Africa. *Environmental Health* 9: 52, pp. 1–13.

Geere, J. L., Mokoena, M. M., Jagals, P., Poland, F., and Hartley, S. 2010b. How do Children Perceive Health to be Affected by Domestic Water Carrying? Qualitative Findings from a Mixed Methods Study in Rural South Africa. *Childcare, Health and Development* 36: 6, pp. 818–26.

Gell, A. 2013. *Art and Agency: an Anthropological Theory*. Oxford: Oxford University Press.

Gibson, J. J. 1977. The Theory of Affordances. In R. Shaw and J. Bransford (eds), *Perceiving, Acting, and Knowing: Toward an Ecological Psychology*. Hillsdale, NJ: Erlbaum, pp. 67–82.

Gilbert, R. 2012. 10 Best Rhod Gilbert Quotes. *WalesOnline* [online]. Available at *http://www.walesonline.co.uk/lifestyle/10-best-rhod-gilbert-quotes-2030129*.

Girón Irueste, F. 2006. Medical Use of Water in the Spanish Early Medieval World (XII–XV Century). In Eyzaguirre, F. M. (ed.) *Balnea: Establecimientos Balnearios: Historia, Literatura y Medicine*. Anejo 1 Serie de Monografía, Publicaciones Universidad Complutense De Madrid.

Gleeson, T., Befus, M. T., Jasechko, S., Luijendijk, E., and Bayani Cardenas, M. 2015. The Global Volume and Distribution of Modern Groundwater. *Nature Geoscience* 9, pp. 161–6 DOI: 10.1038/ngeo2590.

Gleik, P. H. 2014a. Water, Drought, Climate Change and Conflict in Syria. *American Meteorological Society* [online]. Available at *http://journals.ametsoc.org/doi/full/10.1175/WCAS-D-13-00059.1*, pp. 331–40.

Gleik, P. H. (ed.) 2014b. *The World's Water Volume 8*. Island Press.

Gómez-Ortiz, A., Palacios, D., Schulte, L., Salvador-Franch. F., and Plana-Castellvi, J. A. 2009. Evidence from Historical Documents of Landscape Evolution after Little Ice Age of a Mediterranean High Mountain Area, Sierra Nevada, Spain (Eighteenth–Twentieth Centuries). *Physical Geography* 91: 4, pp. 279–89.

Gooley, T. 2016. *How to Read Water: Clues, Signs, Patterns from Puddles to the Sea*. London: Hodder and Stoughton.

GranadaSpain.org. 2017. *http://www.granadaspain.co.uk/what-to-do/what-to-do-in-the-mountains/lanjaron-gateway-to-alpujarra/*.

Greenpeace International. 2016 [online]. Available at *http://www.greenpeace.org/international/en/*.

Griffiths, N. 2007. Wales, England's Oldest Colony: Subjugated and Marginalised, the Welsh have Refused to be Dominated. *New Statesman* [online]. Available at *https://www.newstatesman.com/politics/2007/04/welsh-language-wales-england*.

Gwyndaf, R. 1989. *Welsh Folk Tales*. Cardiff: National Museum of Wales.

Gwyndaf, R. 1992. Folk Legends in Welsh Oral Tradition: Principles of Research, Continuity and Function. Béaloideas, Legends and

Fiction: Papers Presented at the Nordic-Celtic Legend Symposium (1992/1993) Iml: 60/61, pp. 215–40.

Hallis, L. J., Huss, G. R., Nagashima, K., Jeffrey Taylor, G., Halldorsson, S. A., Hilton, D. R., Mott, M. J., and Meech, K. J. 2015. Evidence for Primordial Water in Earth's Deep Mantle. *Science* 350: 6262, pp. 795–7 DOI: 10.1126/science.aac4834.

Haraway, D. 2008. *When Species Meet*. University of Minnesota Press: Minneapolis, London.

Harley, T. A. 2003. The British Obsession with the Weather. In Strauss and Orlove (eds) *Weather, Climate, Culture*. Oxford: Berg, pp. 103–18.

Harris, M. 1979. *Cultural Materialism: the Struggle for a Science of Culture*. AltaMira Press: Walnut Creek, California.

Harvey, G. 2005. *Animism: Respecting the Living World*. Columbia: Columbia University Press.

Headworth, H. G. 2004. Early Arab Water Technology in Southern Spain. *Water and Environment Journal* 18, pp. 161–5. DOI: 10.1111/j.1747-6593.2004.tb00519.x.

Heglund, N. C., Williems, P. A., Penta, M., and Cavagna, G. A. 1995. Energy-saving Gait Mechanics Supported Loads. *Nature* 375, pp. 52–4.

Helmreich, S. 2009. *Alien Ocean: Anthropological Voyages in Microbial Seas*. Berkeley, Los Angeles, London: University of California Press.

Heraclitus. *Heraclitus' Fragments* v. 13.10, Plutarch, Qu. nat. 2, p. 912 [online]. Available at http://www.philaletheians.co.uk/study-notes/hellenic-and-hellenistic-papers/heraclitus'-fragments.pdf.

Herrera Wassilowsky, A. 2011. *La Recuperación de Tecnologías Indígenas: Arqueología, Tecnología y Desarrollo en los Andes*. Bogotá, Universidad de los Andes, CLACSO, IEP.

Hughes, D. M. 2006. Hydrology of Hope: Farm Dams, Conservation, and Whiteness in Zimbabwe. *American Ethnologist* 33: 2, pp. 269–87.

Hurn, S. 2012. *Humans and Other Animals: Human-Animal Interactions in Cross-Cultural Perspective*. London: Pluto Press.

Ingold, T. 2000. *Perceptions of the Environment: Essays on Livelihood, Dwelling and Skill*. London; New York: Routledge.

Ingold, T. 2007. Earth, Sky, Wind and Weather. *Journal of the Royal Anthropological Institute* 13: s1, pp. S19–S38.

Ingold, T. 2011. *Being Alive: Essays on Movement, Knowledge and Description*. Routledge: London.

Ingold, T., and Palsson, G. (eds) 2013. *Biosocial Becomings: Integrating Social and Biological Anthropology*. Cambridge University Press: Cambridge.

InsaneMePlease. 2010. *Cayo – A Documentary on the FWA* [online]. Available at *https://www.youtube.com/watch?v=kF09ynKQQXM*.

Iovino, S., and Oppermann, S. (eds) 2014. *Material Eco-criticism*. Bloomington and Indianapolis: Indiana University Press.

Jeng, M. 2005. How Water can Freeze Faster than Cold?! *Physics* [online]. Available at *https://arxiv.org/pdf/physics/0512262.pdf*, pp. 1–11.

Johnson, B. n.d. Owen Glendower (Owain Glyndŵr) *Historic UK* [online]. Available at *http://www.historic-uk.com/HistoryUK/HistoryofWales/Owen-Glendower-Owain-Glyndwr/*.

Johnston, M. B. 1976. *Dispute Settlement Among the Giriama of Kenya*. PhD thesis presented to the University of Pennsylvania. In Parkin, D. 1991. *The Sacred Void: Spatial Images of Work and Ritual among the Giriama of Kenya*. Cambridge and New York: Cambridge University Press.

Jones, C. A., Davies, S. J., and Macdonald, N. 2012. Examining the Social Consequences of Extreme Weather: the Outcomes of the 1946/1947 Winter in Upland Wales, UK. *Climatic Change* 113, pp. 35–53 DOI: 10.1007/s10584-012-0413-9.

Jones, G. 2017. *Why Not Drown Liverpool? Welsh Water for an English City*. Talk Given for the Liverpool History Society [online]. Available at *http://www.liverpoolhistorysociety.org.uk/wp-content/uploads/2017/09/Why-not-drown-Liverpool-for-Website.pdf*.

Keniger, L. E., Gaston, K. J., Irvine, K. N., and Fuller, R. A. 2013. What are the Benefits of Interacting with Nature? *International Journal of Environmental Research and Public Health* 10: 3, pp. 913–35.

Kirksey, S. E., and Helmreich, S. 2010. The Emergence of a Multispecies Ethnography. *Cultural Anthropology Special Issue: Multispecies Ethnography* 25: 4, pp. 545–76, DOI: 10.1111/j.1548-1360.2010.01069.x.

Kohn, E. 2013. *How Forests Think: Towards an Anthropology of Beyond the Human*. Berkeley, Los Angeles, London: University of California Press.

Kohn, E. 2015. Anthropology of Ontologies. *The Annual Review of Anthropology* 44, pp. 311–27.

Krijtenburg, F. 2013. Keeping This Land Safe: Stakeholder Conceptualisations of Protection in the Context of a Mijikenda (Kenya) World Heritage Site. In Evers, S., Seagle, C., and Krijtenburg, F. *Africa for Sale? Positioning the State, Land and Society in Foreign Large-Scale Land Acquisitions in Africa*. Leiden, Boston: Brill, pp. 275–99.

Lahiri-Dutt, K. 2014. Beyond the Water-Land Binary in Geography: Water/Lands of Bengal Re-visioning Hybridity. *ACME: An International E-Journal for Critical Geographies* 13: 3 pp. 505–29.

Lamb, S. 2000. *White Saris and Sweet Mangoes: Aging, Gender, and Body in North India*. Berkeley: University of California Press.

Lanjaron. n.d. Diputación de Granada [online]. Available at *http://www.turgranada.es/en/municipio/lanjaron/*.

Lansing, S. 1987. Balinese 'Water Temples' and the Management of Irrigation. *American Anthropologist* 89: 2, pp. 326–41.

Lao Tsu. 1989 (trans. Feng, G., English, J., Lippe, T., and Needleman, J.). *Tao Te Ching: Text Only Edition*. Canada, New York: Random House.

Latour, B. 1993a. *We Have Never Been Modern*. Cambridge, MA: Harvard University Press.

Latour, B. 1993b. *The Pasteurization of France*. Cambridge, MA: Harvard University Press.

Latour, B. 2004. *Politics of Nature: How to Bring the Sciences into Democracy*. Cambridge, MA: Harvard University Press.

Latour, B. 2005. *Reassembling the Social: An Introduction to Actor Network Theory*. Oxford, New York: Oxford University Press.

Latour, B. 2014. Agency at the Time of the Anthropocene. *New Literary History* 45, pp. 1–18.

Levi Strauss, C. 1964. *Totemism*, Needham, R. (trans.). London: Merlin Press.

Lloyd, R., Parr, B., Davies, S., Partridge, T., and Cooke, C. 2010. A Comparison of the Physiological Consequences of Head-loading and Back-loading for African and European Women. *European Journal of Applied Physiology* 109: 4, pp. 607–16 DOI: 10.1007/s00421-010-1395-9.

Macdonald, N., Jones, C. A., Davies, S. J., and Charnell-White, C. 2010. Historical Weather Accounts from Wales: An Assessment of their Potential for Reconstructing Climate. *Weather* 65: 3, pp. 72–7.

Madoz, P. 1849. *Diccionario Geografico-Estadistico-Historico de Espana y sus Posesiones de Ultramar*. Tomo XIV (voz Sierra Nevada), pp. 379–86 new edn by Editoriales Andaluzas Unidas-Ambito Valladolid, 1987, p. 302. Cited in Gómez-Ortiz, A., Palacios, D., Schulte, L., Salvador-Franch. F., and Plana-Castellvi, J. A. 2009. Evidence from Historical Documents of Landscape Evolution after Little Ice Age of a Mediterranean High Mountain Area, Sierra Nevada, Spain (Eighteenth-Twentieth Centuries). *Physical Geography* 91A: 4, pp. 279–89.

Malafouris, L. 2013. *How Things Shape the Mind: A Theory of Material Engagement*. Cambridge MA: MIT.

Markale, J. 1976. *Les Celtes et la Civilisation Celtique* Payot Paris Trans. *Celtic Civilisation*. London: Gordon and Cremonesi.

Marletto, C., and Vedral, V. 2017. Witnessing the Quantumness of a System by Observing Only its Classical Features. *Quantum Information* 3: 41, pp. 1–4.

Marriott, M. 1976. Hindu Transactions: Diversity Without Dualism. In *Transaction and Meaning: Directions in the Anthropology of Exchange and Symbolic Behavior* Kapferer, B. (ed.). Philadelphia: Institute for the Study of Human Issues, pp. 109–42.

Martínez, M. T. 2014. *Los Neveros de Sierra Nevada: Historia, Industria y Tradicion (The Snowfield Harvesters of the Sierra Nevada: History, Industry, and Tradition)*. Madrid: Organismo Autónomo Parques Nacionales.

Martínez-Reguera, L. *Bibliografía Hidrológico-Médica Española, Segunda Parte* (Manuscritos y Biografías). Madrid: Sucesores de Rivadeneyra, 2 vols., 1896–97. Cited in Eyzaguirre, F. M. 2006. The Figure of Medical Director in Lanjarón Spa: XIX century. In Eyzaguirre, F. M. (ed.) *Balnea: Establecimientos Balnearios: Historia, Literatura y Medicine*. Anejo 1 Serie de Monografia, Publicaciones Universidad Complutense De Madrid.

Massey, D. 2005. *For Space*. London and Thousand Oaks, CA: Sage.

Mathur, A., and Da Cuhna, D. (eds) 2014. *Design in the Terrain of Water*. California: Point Reyes Station.

Merleau-Ponty, M. 1968. *The Visible and the Invisible*. Evaston: NorthWestern University Press.

Metoffice.gov.uk 2017 [online]. Available at *https://www.metoffice.gov.uk/climate/uk/regional-climates/wl*.

McCully, P. 2001. *Silenced Rivers: The Ecology and Politics of Large Dams*. London, New York: Zed books.
Migues, L. R. 2006. Figuaras Galaicias del Termallismo, in Eyzaguirre, F. M. (ed.), *Balnea: Establecimientos Balnearios: Historia, Literatura y Medicine*. Anejo 1 Serie de Monografia, Publicaciones Universidad Complutense De Madrid, pp. 97–109.
Miller, D. (ed.) 2005. *Materiality*. Duke University Press: Durham and London.
Mitsi, S., and Nicol, A. 2013. *Good Practices in Water Development for Drylands* [online]. Available at http://www.fao.org/fileadmin/user_upload/drought/docs/1_Good%20Practices%20in%20Water%20Development%20for%20Drylands_December%202013.pdf.
Moore, E. B., and Molinero, V. 2011. Structural Transformation in Supercooled Water Controls the Crystallization Rate of Ice. *Nature* 479, pp. 506–9 [online]. Available at https://www.nature.com/articles/nature10586.epdf.
Moran, E. F. 2008. *Human Adaptability: An Introduction to Environmental Anthropology* (3rd edn). Philadelphia: WestView Press.
Morgan, O. 1882. Goldcliff and the Ancient Roman Inscribed Stone Found There. *Monmouthshire and Caerleon Antiquarian Association Papers*, pp. 1–17.
Morgan, T. (Rev.) 1887. Handbook of the Origin of Place-names in Wales and Monmouthshire [online]. Available at http://llennatur.com/files/u1/on_Place-names_ThosMorgan_Pr_HWSouthey_1887.pdf.
Morton, T. 2010. *The Ecological Thought*. Cambridge (MA) and London: Harvard University Press.
Morton, T. 2013. *Hyperobjects: Philosophy and Ecology After the End of the World*. Minneapolis; London: University of Minnesota Press.
Morton, T. 2016. *Dark Ecology: For a Logic of Future Coexistence*. New York: Columbia University Press.
Murillo, P. 1752. *Geographia de Andalucia*. New edition by Biblioteca de Cultura Andaluza. Editoriales Andaluzas Unidas. Sevilla. Cited in Gómez-Ortiz, A., Palacios, D., Schulte, L., Salvador-Franch. F., and Plana-Castellvi, J. A. 2009. Evidence from Historical Documents of Landscape Evolution after Little Ice Age of a Mediterranean High Mountain Area, Sierra Nevada, Spain (Eighteenth-Twentieth Centuries). *Physical Geography*. 91A: 4, pp. 279–89.

Mutoro, H. W. 1985. *The Spatial Distribution of the Mijikenda Kaya Settlements on Hinterland Kenya Coast.* Unpublished PhD thesis. Ann Arbor University, Michigan Bell and Howell Information Co.

Nagle, G. 1998. *Changing Settlements.* Cheltenham: Thomas Nelson and Sons Ltd.

Nair-Venugopal, S., and Paramazivam, S. 2012. 'Indian Collectivism Revisited: Unpacking the Western Gaze'. In *The Gaze of the West and the Framing of the East* Nair-Venugopal, S. (ed.). Hampshire, New York: Palgrave Macmillan, pp. 156–70.

Narby, J. 1998. *The Cosmic Serpent: DNA and the Origins of Knowledge.* New York: Putnam.

Neimanis, A. 2012. We Are All Bodies of Water, II: A Memoir. *Capricious: Water,* Volume 2: Issue No. 13, New York, United States of America: Capricious.

Neimanis, A. 2017. *Bodies of Water: Posthuman Feminist Phenomenology.* London, Oxford, New York: Bloomsbury.

Nilsson, A. 2017. In Stockholm University Press Release Water Exists as Two Different Liquids [online]. Available at *https://www.su.se/english/about/news-and-events/press/press-releases/water-exists-as-two-different-liquids-1.338715*.

Noyes, D. 2003. *Fire in the Placa: Catalan Festival Politics after Franco.* Philadelphia: University of Pennsylvania Press.

Nyamweru, C., Kibet, S., Pakia, M., and Cooke, J. A. 2008. 'The Kaya Forests of Coastal Kenya: "Remnant Patches" or "Dynamic Entities"'. In Sheridan, M. J., and Nuamweru, C. *African Sacred Groves.* Oxford: James Currey, pp. 62–86.

Online Etymology Dictionary 2018 [online]. Available at *www.etymonline.com/index.php?term=influence*.

Osmond, J. 2009. Cofiwch Dryweryn [online]. Available at *http://www.iwa.wales/click/2009/08/cofiwch-dryweryn/*.

Oswald, A. 2012. Liquid Rules of Sympathy. *New Statesman* [online]. Available at *www.newstatesman.com/lifestyle/2012/04/liquid-rules-sympathy*.

Palmer, L. 2015. *Water Politics and Spiritual Ecology: Custom, Environmental Governance and Development.* London: Routledge.

Parkin, D. 1991. *The Sacred Void: Spatial Images of Work and Ritual among the Giriama of Kenya.* Cambridge and New York: Cambridge University Press.

Ponz, A. 1797. *Relacion del Viaje que Desde Granada Hizo a Sierra Nevada D. Antonio Ponz a Influxo del Excmo. Sr. Marques de la Ensena Mensajero Economico y Erudite de Granada*. Cited in Gómez-Ortiz, A., Palacios, D., Schulte, L., Salvador-Franch. F., and Plana-Castellvi, J. A. 2009. Evidence from Historical Documents of Landscape Evolution after Little Ice Age of a Mediterranean High Mountain Area, Sierra Nevada, Spain (Eighteenth–Twentieth Centuries). *Physical Geography* 91A: 4, pp. 279–89.

Porter, G., Hampshire, K., Dunn, C. Hall, R., Levesley, M. Burton, B., Robson, S., Abane, A., Blell, M., and Panther, P. 2013. Health Impacts of Pedestrian Head-loading: A Review of the Evidence with Particular Reference to Women and Children in Sub-Saharan Africa. *Social Science & Medicine* 88, pp. 90–7.

Purpura, A. 2009. Framing the Ephemeral. *African Arts* 42: 3, Ephemeral Arts 1, pp. 11–21.

Rainbird, P. 2007. *The Archaeology of Islands*. Cambridge: Cambridge University Press.

Ramberg, L., Wolski, P., and Krah, M. 2006. Water Balance and Infiltration in the Okavango Delta, Botswana. *Wetlands* 26: 3, pp. 677–90.

Richards, V. 2010. The Village Drowned to Give Another Nation Water *Independent* [online]. Available at *http://www.independent.co.uk/news/uk/this-britain/the-village-drowned-to-give-another-nation-water-2108977.html*.

Riebeek, H. 2008. *The Ocean's Carbon Balance* [online]. Available at *https://earthobservatory.nasa.gov/Features/OceanCarbon/*.

Rightsofnature.org. 2010. *Final Universal Declaration of the Rights of Mother Earth* [online]. Available at *http://therightsofnature.org/wp-content/uploads/pdfs/FINAL-UNIVERSAL-DECLARATION-OF-THE-RIGHTS-OF-MOTHER-EARTH-APRIL-22-2010.pdf*.

Rowlands, D. W. L. 2005. *The Policeman's Story: Special Constable David Jones's reminiscences about Old Llanddwyn and the Construction of Lake Vyrnwy*. St Wddyn's Parochial Church Council: WPG Press.

Rowling, M 2017. Thirsty World Must Wake up to Looming Water Crisis, Expert Says. *Reuters* [online]. Available at *https://www.reuters.com/article/us-global-water-development/thirsty-world-must-wake-up-to-looming-water-crisis-expert-says-idUSKCN1B41V4*.

Samos, J. P. 2006. El Agua Como Recurso Turístico en un Entorno Rural: el Balneario de Lanjarón. In Eyzaguirre, F. M (ed.) *Balnea: Establecimientos Balnearios: Historia, Literatura y Medicine*. Anejo 1 Serie de Monografia, Publicaciones Universidad Complutense De Madrid.

Schwenk, T. 2014. *Sensitive Chaos: the Creation of Flowing Forms in Water and Air*. East Sussex: Sophia Books.

Serres, M. 1992. Natural Contract. *Critical Inquiry* 17: 3, pp. 1–215.

Shaw, S., and Francis, A. 2014. *Deep Blue: Critical Reflections on Nature, Religion and Water*. London: Routledge.

Sheldrake, R. 2004. *The Sense of Being Stared at: And Other Aspects of the Extended Mind*. London: Random House, Arrow Books.

Smith, A. 2007. *The Oxford Companion to American Food and Drink*. Oxford: Oxford University Press.

Spear, T. T. 1978. *The Kaya Complex: A History of the Mijikenda Peoples of the Kenya Coast to 1900*. Nairobi: Kenya Literature Bureau.

Stephens, M. 2009. Cited in Osmond, J. 2009. *Cofiwch Dryweryn* [online]. Available at *http://www.iwa.wales/click/2009/08/cofiwch-dryweryn/*.

Stockholm University Press Office, 2017. *Water Exists as Two Different Liquids* [online]. Available at *https://www.su.se/english/about/news-and-events/press/press-releases/water-exists-as-two-different-liquids-1.338715*.

Strang, V. 2004. *The Meaning of Water*. Oxford, New York: Berg/Bloomsbury.

Strang, V. 2009. *Gardening the World: Agency, Identity and the Ownership of Water*. New York, Oxford: Berghahn.

Strang, V. 2010. The Summoning of Dragons: Ancestral Serpents and Indigenous Water Rights in Australia and New Zealand. *Anthropology News* 51: 2, pp. 5–7.

Strang, V. 2013a. Conceptual Relations: Water, Ideologies, and Theoretical Subversions. In Chen, C., MacLeod, J., and Neimanis, A. *Thinking with Water*. Montreal and Kingston, London, Ithaca: McGill-Queen's University Press, pp. 185–212.

Strang, V. 2013b. Going Against the Flow: The Biopolitics of Dams and Diversions. *Worldviews: Global Religions, Culture, and Ecology*, 17: 2, pp. 161–70.

Strang, V. 2014. Fluid Consistencies. Material relationality in human engagements with water. *Archaeological Dialogues*, 21: 2, pp. 133–50.
Strang, V. 2015. *Water: Nature and Culture*. Reaktion Books: London.
Strang, V. 2016. Re-imagined Communities: A New Ethical Approach to Water Policy. In *The Oxford Handbook of Water Politics and Policy* Conca, C., and Weinthal, E. Oxford, New York: Oxford University Press, pp. 142–67.
Strathern, M. 1999. *Property, Substance and Effect: Anthropological Essays on Persons and Things*. London: Continuum.
Swyngedouw, E. 2015. *Liquid Power: Contested Hydro-Modernities in Twentieth-Century Spain*. Cambridge, MA: MIT Press.
Thomas. R. S. 2000. *R. S. Thomas: Collected Poems: 1945–1990*. London: Phoenix Books.
Thomas, W. 2013. *Hands off Wales: Nationhood and Militancy*. Llandysul, Ceredigion: Gomer Press.
Tibballs, G. 2010. *The Bowler's Holding, the Batsman's Willey: The Greatest Collection of Humorous Sporting Quotations Ever!* Chester: Ebury Press.
Trafford, B. D. 1970. Field Drainage. *Journal of the Royal Agricultural Society* 131, pp. 129–52.
Tsing, A. L. 2015. *The Mushroom at the End of the World: On the Possibility of Life in Capitalist Ruins*. Princeton and Oxford: Princeton Books.
Turnbull, T. 1987. *The Forest People*. New York: Simon and Schuster.
UNESCO. 2008. The World Heritage Convention Nomination Dossier for Inscription on the World Heritage List: *The Sacred Mijikenda Kaya Forests* (Kenya) [online]. Available at http://whc.unesco.org/uploads/nominations/1231rev.pdf.
UNESCO. 2016. Sacred Mijikenda Kaya Forests [online]. Available at http://whc.unesco.org/en/list/1231.
UNESCO-MAB. 2007. Biosphere Reserve Information: Spain, Sierra Nevada *UNESCO MAB Biosphere Reserve Directory* [online]. Available at http://www.unesco.org/mabdb/br/brdir/directory/biores.asp?mode=all&code=SPA+10.
UNSDG. n.d. Sustainable Development Knowledge Platform: Sustainable Development Goals *United Nations* [online]. Available at https://sustainabledevelopment.un.org/?menu=1300.
UN-water 2014 [online]. Available at http://www.unwater.org.

Urry, J. 2005. The Complexity Turn *Theory, Culture & Society* 22:5, pp. 1–14 DOI: 10.1177/0263276405057188.

Van Dooren, T. 2016. The Unwelcome Crows: Hospitality in the Anthropocene. *Angelaki: Journal of the Theoretical Humanities* 21: 2, pp. 193–212.

Van Gennep, A. 2004. *The Rites of Passage*. London, New York: Routledge.

Vokes, R. (ed.) 2013. *Photography in Africa: Ethnographic Perspectives*. Suffolk: James Currey.

WalesOnline. 2012. No Hosepipe Ban for Wales Yet, but England Wilts [online]. Available at *http://www.walesonline.co.uk/news/local-news/no-hosepipe-ban-yet-wales-2044745*.

Wanza, N. C., and Mugwima, B. N. 2012. *Designing for Sustainability in Cultural Landscapes: the Kaya Kinondo Forest of the Mijikenda Community, Kenya Sustainable Futures: Architecture and Urbanism in the Global South*. Kampala, Uganda.

Wagner, J. R. (ed.) 2015. *The Social Life of Water*. New York, Oxford: Berg.

Weir, R. 2015. The History of Ice Cream. *ICA.org* [online]. Available at *https://www.ice-cream.org/content/history-ice-cream*.

Welsh Government. 2017a. *Welsh Landscapes* [online]. Available at *http://www.wales.com/welsh-landscapes*.

Welsh Government. 2017b. *Where is Wales* [online]. Available at *http://www.wales.com/where-is-wales*.

Whatmore, S. 2002. *Hybrid Geographies: Natures Cultures Spaces*. Sage, London.

Wilkens, A., Jacobi, M., and Schwenk, W. 2005. *Understanding Water: Developments From the Work of Theodor Schwenk*. Edinburgh: Floris Books.

Williams. O. 2016. *Tryweryn: A Nation Awakes*. Ceredigion: Y Lolfa Cyf.

Willis, J., and Miers, S. 1997. Becoming a Child of the House: Incorporation, Authority and Resistance in Giryama Society. *Journal of African History* 38, pp. 479–95.

Wilson, A. I. 2004. Classical Water Technology in the Early Islamic World. In C. Bruun and A. Saastamoinen (eds). *Technology, Ideology, Water: from Frontinus to the Renaissance and Beyond* (Acta Instituti Romani Finlandiae, 31), Roma, pp. 115–41.

Witmore, C. 2014. Archaeology and the New Materialisms. *Journal of Contemporary Archaeology* 1, pp. 203–46.

Witmore, C. 2015. Archaeology, Symmetry and the Ontology of Things. A Response to Critics. *Archaeological Dialogues* 22, pp. 187–97.

Wittfogel, K.A. 1957. *Oriental Despotism: A Comparative Study of Power*. New Haven and London: Yale University Press.

Wright, J. B., and Campbell, C. L. 2008. Moorish Cultural Landscapes of Las Alpujarras. *Focus on Geography* 51: 1, pp. 25–30.

WWAP, 2018. *WWAP (United Nations World Water Assessment Programme) The United Nations World Water Development Report 2018: Nature-based Solutions*. Paris, UNESCO [online]. Available at http://www.unesco.org/new/en/natural-sciences/environment/water/wwap/wwdr/2018-nature-based-solutions/.

Wyn James, E. 2005. Painting the World Green: Dafydd Iwan and the Welsh Protest Ballad. *Folk Music Journal* 8: 5, pp. 594–618.

Zeleza, T. 1995. *Mijikenda*. New York: Rosen Publishing Group.

INDEX

A
Acequia 102, 111, 112
Actor 12, 51, 59, 113, 145
Actor Network Theory (ANT) 12, 38, 59
Agency x, 12, 13, 38, 42, 53, 55, 59, 84, 86, 130
Andalusia 60, 66, 94, 109
Anthropocene, Age of 6, 14, 127, 128
Aquifer 70, 96, 101–3
Astrology 21
Ayurveda 21

B
Biology (biological) 14, 16, 29, 44, 62, 128, 146, 147
Biophysical 50, 51
Bodies 3, 4, 8, 10–17, 20, 28, 32, 33, 38, 40, 43–6, 53–6, 60–1, 67, 68, 71, 73, 74,77, 81, 82, 90–3, 108, 111–12, 115, 116, 124, 147
Bridewealth 72, 78

C
Capitalism 21
Carbon 19–20
Carbon dioxide 37, 70
Cartesian 5
    Cartesian Cut 8
Climate(s) 37, 70, 94, 95, 99, 100, 117, 124, 134
    Change 47, 114, 121
Comets 23

Communication 32, 82–3
Compounds 19
Coriolis Effect 36
Culture(s) 9, 11, 15, 16, 20, 25, 55, 60, 77, 86, 95, 119, 127, 135, 138, 141, 144
    Culture and nature; nature/culture 16, 55, 56
    Material culture ix, 8, 60

D
Dam (dammed, damming) 17, 36, 53, 55–6, 115–16, 129–33,136, 139, 142, 144, 148
Deposition 35, 104
Dividial 89
Drought 16, 65, 68, 71
Dry 12, 31, 54, 69, 70, 91, 93, 95, 99, 100, 102–3, 110–11
    Ground, dry 31
    Dry, wet and 12
Dwelling 65, 77

E
Ecocriticism 21
    -critical 42
    -material/ity 56, 145
    -pluralist 13
Ecological 5, 9, 49–53, 59, 60, 62, 93, 102
Element(al) 4, 21, 39, 40, 42, 113
England 117, 126–9, 132, 134, 135, 144, 145

English 47, 115, 122, 123, 129, 132–4, 137–9, 141–4, 148
Erosion 35

F
Festival (see also Fiesta) 60, 113, 114, 147
Fiesta 109, 113
Flood (see also Water) 17, 23, 36
Flow see Water
   Flow, air 117
Form 8, 60, 61
Freeze (frozen) 17, 27–33, 40, 94, 97, 98, 108, 147
Fu ha mwenga 76–81, 89

G
Gender 71, 72
Giriama 60, 65–6, 68–92, 95, 100, 125, 147
Glacial 96, 97, 99, 102, 104
   Glacier 23, 46, 96
Glass 25, 28
   Bottle 129
Gyres 36

H
Harambee 80
Head carrying 71–5
Hot springs 104
Human exceptionalism/ist 9, 14, 51, 146
Hybrid(ity) 13, 31, 52
Hydrogen 19, 21–3, 26–30, 33, 98
Hydrography 15
   -culture 100
   -graphers 100
   -graphic 45, 47
   -philic 38
Hyperobjects 20, 40

I
Ice see water
   -cream 97
Identity 66, 67, 69, 71, 76, 78, 82–4, 89, 91, 92, 127, 133, 138, 141–3, 147
Intra
   -action/activity 39
   -relational 13

K
Kaya (see also MaKaya) 85–8
Kenya 16, 65–70, 80, 82–3, 86–7, 93, 123, 144, 147
Kinship 78, 86

L
Lake 29, 96, 100, 118, 124–5, 129–30, 132, 137
Land 6, 16, 23, 31, 34, 38, 50, 54, 69, 70, 85, 91, 100, 102, 103, 116–17, 121, 124–8, 131–3, 138–40, 142–4, 147
   -scape(s) 15, 17, 35, 37, 40, 45, 51, 53, 66–8, 70, 82–3, 88, 91–9, 101, 103, 108, 120, 124–6, 133, 135, 143–4, 147
   Farmland 80, 127, 135
Lanjaron 66, 93–5, 98–101, 104–9, 112–14, 147
Liquid 3, 18, 23, 24–30, 32–5, 40, 44–5, 83, 84, 86, 91, 98, 111, 113–16

M
Makaya 86–8
Mijikenda 69, 81, 86–7, 88
Molecule 13, 20, 24, 27, 29, 30, 34, 44, 98, 124
   Molecularity, disordered 27

Moors (Moorish) 66, 96, 98–100, 105, 107
Moors, Welsh 120, 122
More-than-human 4, 13, 24, 48, 50, 59
Movement (moving) 55, 56, 75, 82
   of neck and body 74, 75
   Seismic 108
   of snow 120
   of water 16, 23, 26, 33–8, 44–5, 49–50, 67, 96, 98, 109, 116, 123, 135
   Welsh nationalist 136–7, 139, 144
Multispecies 12, 13, 48

N
Nature-based solutions (NBS) 51–3
Nature (see also Culture) 16, 24, 33, 41, 43, 51, 54–6, 99, 115

O
Ocean(s) 22, 23, 31, 33–4, 45, 46, 62, 87, 117
   Waves, ocean 37
Oceanic gyres 36
Ontology 3, 5, 6, 39, 42, 50, 146
   Relational ontology 5, 39, 42, 50, 146
Oxygen 5, 19, 21, 22, 23, 26–7, 29–30, 33

P
Person 11, 14, 74, 77, 89
   Personal(ly) 47, 67, 76, 79, 80
   Personhood 15, 90
Physics 4–6, 23, 24, 26, 60, 147
   Physics, quantum 13
Posthumanism 13, 48
Postmodernism 59

Q
Quantum physics 13

R
Rain(s) 23, 29, 34, 45
Relational ontology see Ontology
Reservoir 45, 129–32, 134–41, 144
Resource(s) 5, 6, 9, 18, 47, 48, 49, 52–4, 57, 59, 61, 83, 115, 116, 127, 143–44
Riparian zone 38–9
Ritual 65, 67, 76, 83, 87–9, 95, 109–14, 147
   Ritualized actions 81
River 23, 25, 35, 36, 38, 39, 44, 45, 53, 56, 69, 71, 73, 76, 81, 83, 95–6, 101, 115, 119, 122–3, 127, 129–32
   Dee, River 137
   Guadalfeo, River 104
   Koromi, River 70
   Tryweryn, River 135
   of people, river 112
   Rights of rivers 15
   Seasonal 69–70
   River, space of a 44

S
Singwaya 81–2, 87–8
Snow 17, 23, 32, 66, 93–4, 96–9, 102, 104, 109, 114, 117, 120–1
Spa 105
Space ix, 4, 21, 26, 27, 28, 46, 79, 87–8, 108, 111
   Space, water in 23, 34
   Occupying space 30–1, 32
   Space as a river 44
   Space and place 145
   Space, cultural 55
   Space, liminal 32

Spain 17, 66, 93–4, 98–9, 101, 104–5, 107, 109–10, 123, 147, 149
Spherical (drop) (see also Water) 33–6
Spiral (see also Water) 34–6, 38, 44–5
Spiritual 30, 41
Spring 49, 66, 101, 102–7, 119, 123, 126
Steam see water
Stream(s) 23, 34–6, 69, 110–11

T
Temperature(s) 17, 21, 26–9, 33, 35–7, 71, 92, 96–7, 114, 120
Topography 23, 30, 98
Tsunami 23, 40, 113, 125
Transport 16, 30–3, 40, 89, 91, 97, 127
Tryweryn 132, 134–6, 140

U
Ubunte 80

W
Wales 17, 117–27, 129, 132–45, 147
    Wet, Wales 67, 117, 122
Water
    Drop, of, droplets 20, 29, 33, 34, 40, 101, 110, 117, 122
    Flood(ing) 17, 23, 36, 47, 53, 67, 69, 71, 99, 108, 110, 117, 119, 120, 121, 124, 125, 130–3, 139–41, 144, 147
    Flows 3, 5, 9, 10, 11, 12, 14, 18, 19, 26, 30, 32–5, 38–47, 50, 53, 54, 55, 56, 58, 60, 62, 66, 69, 70, 71, 75, 95, 96, 98, 99, 104, 110–12, 114–16, 123, 132, 146, 147

Glacial 96, 99, 102, 104
    Ice, glacial 97, 99
Groundwater 101
Ice 22, 23, 27–9, 32–3, 60, 96–9, 109
    Dead ice 96
    Glacial ice 97, 99
Invisible 18, 47, 101, 102
Mineral 66, 67, 97, 104–8, 119, 147
Pure 30–1, 108
    Ultra-pure 30–1
Slow 17, 67, 93, 96, 98, 101
Space, water in 23, 34
Spherical 35–6
    Drop 33
    Water molecule 34
Spiral(ling) 34–6, 44–5
Steam 23, 25, 29, 32, 34, 35, 127, 128
Supercooled 28
Transform(ing/ation) 15, 19, 22, 23, 25–6, 28, 31–4, 39, 41, 43–4, 56
Weight of 34, 35, 67, 73–5, 115–16, 144
Waterfall(s) 40, 118, 119, 131
Watertable 69, 70
Watershed 69
Waves 29, 34, 37, 38, 125
Weight see Water
Welsh(ness) 67, 115–48
Wet 25, 48, 91, 93, 102, 132
    Wet theory 12, 48, 54
    Wet, Wales 67, 117, 122
    Wetter, wetness 38, 58, 100, 110–11, 116, 122